1895 & ALL THAT...

Tony Collins

1895 & ALL THAT...

Inside Rugby League's
Hidden History

Scratching Shed Publishing Ltd

First published by Scratching Shed Publishing Ltd in 2009
Registered in England & Wales No. 6588772.
Registered office:
47 Street Lane, Leeds, West Yorkshire. LS8 1AP

www.scratchingshedpublishing.co.uk

ISBN 978-0956007599

Unless stated otherwise, all photographs are from the personal collection
of Tony Collins or the Rugby Football League archive

A catalogue record for this book is available from the British Library.

Typeset in Warnock Pro Semi Bold and Palatino

Printed and bound in the United Kingdom by
L.P.P.S.Ltd, Wellingborough, Northants, NN8 3PJ

'I say with Mark Twain's bold, bad boy, that we glory in the sentence of outlawry pronounced on us, as freeing us from the tyrannical bondage of the English [Rugby] Union, and we breath pure air in being freed from the stifling atmosphere of deceit in which we previously existed.'
- *letter to the 'Yorkshire Post', 21 September 1895*

Contents

Harold Wagstaff

1

Introduction

'I am a Northern Union man through and through', wrote Harold Wagstaff in his 1935 autobiography.

Modernise Northern Union to rugby league and this is a sentiment that has been shared by tens of thousands of rugby league supporters in the decades since Wagstaff wrote these words.

Part of the reason why they share this credo - whether they watch the game in Golborne or Goroka, Carcassonne or Cabramatta - is because of the history of rugby league. No sport has a history like that of rugby league. Born in the massive expansion of sport and leisure in late Victorian England, the game has survived and thrived despite the huge obstacles put in its way by its opponents.

This book uncovers some of the hidden and forgotten parts of rugby league history. The early part of the book looks at the personalities and the politics of the 1895 split that gave rise to the Northern Union. But it also digs deep to explore the origins of the split between rugby and soccer, the role of black players in rugby league and the crucial part played by Australia in the development of the British game over the last hundred or so years.

Although this is a book aimed at the rugby league fan, anyone interested in the history of sport will get something out of it. Each chapter has been adapted - some more, some less - from a variety of articles that I have published in academic history journals over the past fifteen years. Academic journals tend be very expensive, often jargon-laden, and usually not easy for non-academics to access. So I have tried to cut out the more obscure passages in these chapters and make them more directly relevant to the non-academic reader without sacrificing quality.

For those who would like to delve further into the topics in this book, references to the original articles can be found in the notes to each chapter. And, of course, the themes of this book are discussed in much greater detail in my trilogy on the history of rugby: *Rugby's Great Split*, *Rugby League in Twentieth Century Britain* and *A Social History of English Rugby Union*.

The historian Eric Hobsbawm once wrote that, for the black American musicians who created and played it, jazz was: 'a continuous means of asserting oneself as a human being, as an agent in the world and not the subject of others' actions, as a discipline of the soul, a daily testing, an expression of the value and sense of life, a way to perfection'.

As this book aims to prove, much the same can be said about rugby league.

TONY COLLINS
JUNE 2009

The England rugby team - 1894
Captain Dicky Lockwood is pictured centre, holding ball

Dicky Lockwood

2

The Greatest Player You've Never Heard Of

In the conclusion to his wonderful book *The Great Ones*, Eddie Waring regrets that he did not have more space to talk about other great players. In particular, he mentions one name, his father's favourite player: Dewsbury's Dicky Lockwood.

Lockwood is probably the greatest player that most fans of rugby (of either code) have never heard of. Yet his achievements in rugby before the 1895 split are unrivalled. But despite his unparalleled feats as a player, he has been excluded from the pantheon of Victorian and Edwardian rugby immortality. This chapter aims to set the record straight, and in doing so, offer an explanation for his disappearance from rugby history.[1]

A brief glimpse of his career should be enough to convince anyone of his greatness. He made his debut for England in 1887 at the age of nineteen as a wing-threequarter. He equalled E.T. Gurdon's record of fourteen England caps and would have received many more if the Rugby Football Union had not clashed with the

International Board and refused to play in Four Nations matches in 1888 and 1889.

In an age in which tries were not common and matches were low-scoring affairs, he scored five tries and kicked seven conversions in an England shirt. In 1894 he captained England to one of their greatest victories when they routed Wales using the Principality's own four three-quarter system for the first time.

If mere statistics do not prove his greatness, a glance at how the rugby correspondents of the *Yorkshire Post* described his international performances should convince.

On his debut against Wales: 'Lockwood stood out a bright and shining light.'

Against the touring 1888 Maoris: 'his display being such as to stamp him as the best three-quarter on the ground'.

Playing against Ireland in 1891: 'the most finished player on the ground... his sure tackling only exceeded by his sprinting, which reached the highest standard of excellence'.

In 1892 against Wales at Richmond: 'played a grand game ... was seen quite at his best on the defence'.

And from the same year in England's defeat of Scotland in Edinburgh:

> 'Lockwood was playing like three ordinary backs rolled into one [on defence] ... Never has more judicious wing-play been displayed. He was at once smart and even brilliant: safe, and most effective. Whatever he did, he did well; and whether it was running or dropping, saving or tackling, he was good at one and all these points alike'.[2]

On this evidence alone, Dicky Lockwood was unquestionably the most outstanding English back of his day - only Welsh captain and rival centre Arthur Gould could compare. Yet he has been forgotten. The official centenary history of the Rugby Football Union (RFU) doesn't even mention him while O.L. Owen's earlier book on the RFU notes him only in passing and doesn't refer to his captaincy of England.

The World's Wonder

Richard Evison Lockwood was born on 11 November 1867 to a labouring family in Crigglestone, near Wakefield.

His rugby career began at the age of sixteen for Dewsbury - then one of the North's leading sides - when he made his debut on the right wing against Ossett in November 1884, a few days before his seventeenth birthday. In those days most English sides played with just three three-quarters but Dicky could play on the wing or in the centres with equal accomplishment.

He quickly became a phenomenon and was nicknamed 'the Little Tyke' and 'Little Dick, the World's Wonder', partly because of his youth and also because of his diminutive stature - he was only five feet, four and a half inches tall. Even at an early age he was the complete footballer, brilliant in attack, deadly in the tackle and precise in his kicking, with a knack of being in the right place at the right time.

In 1886 he was selected for the first of his forty-six appearances for the Yorkshire county side and shortly after his nineteenth birthday he played for the North against the South, an annual match that was a trial for England selection.

Even at this stage his fame was such that crowds gathered in Dewsbury market place to hear telegram reports from the match being read out. The following month, in January 1887, he made his England debut versus Wales at Llanelli: 'Lockwood ... won golden encomiums from everybody,' was how one newspaper reported his sensational debut.[3]

Dicky-mania quickly engulfed the Dewsbury area, demonstrating that sporting stardom and fan hysteria were not born in the 1960s. Leaving Dewsbury's Crown Flatt ground after a blinding display in a Yorkshire Cup tie against Wakefield Trinity, the weekly *Yorkshireman* reported that Lockwood 'was mobbed by a vast crowd which, contracting as the road narrowed, actually pushed down a strong stone wall and then shoved a hawker and a little lad through the aperture into the field below'.[4]

Pictures of Dicky were sold outside of the ground and by photographers' shops in Dewsbury itself, one enterprising trader charging one shilling and a penny per photo, almost one-eighth of the nine shillings weekly wage the player himself then received as a woollen printer in Walmsley's local textile mill. Playing in Dublin against Ireland in February 1887 he was carried off with a broken collar bone, filling Dewsbury with wild rumours that he had actually been killed in the match. Hundreds waited through the night at Dewsbury railway station to see him come home from the game, just to prove to themselves that their 'Little Wonder' was still alive.

In 1889 Dicky shocked his fans and left Dewsbury to play for Heckmondwike, a mill town a few miles down the road, which, thanks to an aggressive policy of attracting players through match payments and jobs, boasted one of the best teams in the county, which included England players such as the forward Donald Jowett and three-quarter John Sutcliffe, one of the few men to be capped by England at both soccer and rugby. Although his ostensible reason for moving was to play for a better team, it was widely reported that he had told friends that 'he had got all he could out of Dewsbury and that he was going to Heckmondwike to see what he could get there'. Contrary to RFU's strict amateur regulations, he allegedly received one pound per match to play for the club and was given the tenancy of The Queen's Hotel pub in Heckmondwike.

Such blatant flouting of the amateur regulations was too much for the Yorkshire rugby union, who were in the middle of attempting to exorcise the professional devil from their midst. Dicky was investigated by the Yorkshire Rugby Union (YRU) about his transfer to see if any money had changed hands or promises of work been made. Being unable to find any direct evidence, the YRU found him not guilty of the charge of being a professional. That night in Heckmondwike, the *Yorkshireman* reported that 'hundreds of people collected in the market place and its approaches, and the news of his acquittal was received with an outburst of cheering, the gathering in all respects resembling those witnessed at an exciting political election.'[5]

Undaunted, the YRU then charged the Heckmondwike club with directly paying players. The YRU had overwhelming circumstantial evidence against the club. Its accounts showed that gate money from the grandstand always came to an even amount and that, despite having a successful side with three England internationals in it, in only two games during the previous season did they take more than £20 at the gate. Not only did they not have a bank account but the treasurer confessed that he never counted the gate money. Further questions were also raised as to how three players who had transferred to Heckmondwike all worked at the same dyeing factory in the town. Eventually the club and its players were suspended for three months.[6]

But worse was to come for Dicky. In December he was again summoned to appear before the YRU committee, where he was charged once more with professionalism and cross-examined by the Reverend Frank Marshall, headmaster of Almondbury school and leading YRU official. Marshall claimed that Morley tried to induce Dicky to transfer to them in 1886 with an offer of an apprenticeship but that Dewsbury kept him by offering 10s a week and £1 per exhibition match.

The 'trial' lasted for three days and Dicky showed an admirable talent for stonewalling, as the follow extracts from the cross-examination shows:

> **Marshall:** 'What year were you asked to go to Morley?'
> **Lockwood:** '1886 about.'
> **Marshall:** 'What was the inducement?'
> **Lockwood:** 'Nothing.'
> **Marshall:** 'Do you know Mr Crabtree of Morley?'
> **Lockwood:** 'Yes.'
> **Marshall:** 'What did he offer you?'
> **Lockwood:** 'He did not offer to apprentice me to him. I was not paid anything. If anyone stated I was paid it would be wrong.'
> **Marshall:** 'A gentleman has stated that you were paid 10s a week.'
> **Lockwood:** 'Well, that gentleman is wrong.' ...
> **Marshall:** 'I want you to be very particular about this. I have positive information that you were paid after refusing to go to Morley.'
> **Lockwood:** 'I was not, sir.'
> **Marshall:** 'I understand you were paid £1 for exhibition matches.'
> **Lockwood:** 'That is wrong.'
> **Marshall:** 'Were you in a position to go to these matches and lose your wages?'

Lockwood: 'Then I was, sir.' ...
Marshall: 'I want to be explicit on this point, as to the meaning of 'dinners'. Have you ever been told that, seeing that you were not so well off, you could have 'dinners' if you went to play with any club?'
Lockwood: 'No, never.'[7]

It was examples such as this which eventually led the RFU to change its rules and switch the burden of proof to the accused in cases of alleged professionalism. Needless to say, unable to penetrate Dicky's defence, the YRU committee simply gave up and acquitted him yet again. The one practical impact of the trial was that he was not selected for England that season, as international matches resumed after the ending of the RFU's dispute with the International Board.

Nevertheless, controversy still dogged his career. Unlike his nearest equivalent of the time as a regional sporting hero, Arthur Gould, Dicky was unambiguously working class, a serious handicap to gaining the respect of those who ran the game: 'Dicky doesn't sport sufficient collar and cuff for the somewhat fastidious members of the committee,' the rugby writer of the *Yorkshireman* reported in 1891. The tension between Dicky and the game's authorities epitomised the relationship between the supporters of amateurism who ran the game and working class players who had come to dominate its playing. In 1891 he was passed over for the Yorkshire county captaincy in favour of Oxford-educated William Bromet. 'It is simply a case of pandering to social position, nothing more nor less. We thought we were 'all fellows at football'; yet an alleged democratic Yorkshire committee can still show a sneaking fondness for persons who are... we had almost said in a better social position than ourselves' complained the same correspondent.[8]

Eventually talent did prevail and in 1892 Dicky was chosen as the captain of the Yorkshire county side, leading them to a hat-trick of county championships over the next three years. His captaincy was notable for more than just his continuation of Yorkshire dominance of the county championship. He helped to implement the Welsh system of playing with four three-quarters. Previously the dominance of northern forwards meant that clubs were reluctant to move to the four three-quarter system first used by the Welsh national side in 1886. 'Buller' Stadden had unsuccessfully introduced the system to Dewsbury when he moved there from Cardiff in 1886, but Oldham were the first northern side to use it regularly when Bill McCutcheon joined them in 1888 from Swansea. Even then, there was still widespread doubt in Lancashire and Yorkshire as to its usefulness - despite northern admiration for the back play of Welsh clubs like Newport, it was believed that its success in Wales was due to the poorer quality of Welsh forward play, especially in comparison to club football in the north of England. When it came to be widely, although not universally, accepted in England in the early 1890s, it was partly due to Lockwood's influence and the success of the Yorkshire side in using the new system.[9]

Dicky's unique combination of all-round skill and tactical innovation reached their highest point in 1894, when he was chosen to captain England against Wales at Birkenhead. Playing with four three-quarters for the first time, the English side routed Wales at their own game, winning by 24 points to 3, the highest score by England since the very first Anglo-Welsh game in 1881. It was, said the *Liverpool Mercury*, 'not a beating, it was an annihilation'. Dicky himself scored a try and kicked three conversions, totally outplaying his opposite number Arthur Gould. The most potent factor in this historic victory, according to the

Yorkshire Post, 'was Lockwood, who covered Gould with merciless persistency, and in all his long career Lockwood has never played with greater judgement or effect'.[10]

Even more significant than the victory was Lockwood's personal achievement in becoming captain of England. Rugby was led on and off the field by middle class ex-public school boys, yet here was an unskilled manual labourer with little secondary education leading men who were, according to all of society's norms at the time, several times his social superior. It was almost as if a conscript private had taken charge of an elite cavalry regiment. His captaincy symbolised the rise of the working class player in rugby, something which many in rugby's hierarchy had steadfastly vowed to oppose.

The month after the defeat of Wales, he captained the national side against Ireland at Blackheath, only to go down to defeat by 7 points to 5. Badly hampered by a lack of possession, Dicky scored England's only try of the match by charging down a kick from the Irish full-back Sparrow, a try acclaimed as: 'one of the finest pieces of work in the direction of taking advantage of an opponent's weakness ever seen in first-class football'. Although no-one knew at the time, this was to be not only his last appearance as England captain, but also his last appearance in any type of representative football.[11]

Shortly after the Ireland match he informed the English selectors that he would not be available for the Calcutta Cup match in Edinburgh because he couldn't afford to take time off work to travel up to Scotland and back. Despite this, he asked the RFU for permission to play for Heckmondwike in a home game taking place on the same day. The Rugby Union refused point-blank to allow him to play for his club - despite the fact Eton house master Cyril Wells had been allowed in similar circumstances to play for Harlequins after pulling out of the Rest of England team beaten by Yorkshire the previous season.

This caused a considerable furore in Yorkshire, where it was seen as gross hypocrisy on the part of the RFU and one more example of how working class players were treated differently from those with a public school background.

The affair added yet more impetus to the calls for working class players to be paid broken time money to compensate for time lost at work due to playing rugby. Disgusted with the RFU and by the Yorkshire Rugby Union's failure to support him fully, Lockwood announced his retirement from representative football for both England and Yorkshire. Years later, he hinted that he thought he may have been the victim of a conspiracy, commenting that 'there was always a strong feeling against us' on the part of the RFU leadership.[12]

Dicky therefore came to embody the growing crisis that was engulfing English rugby union and which would lead to the 1895 split. Working class players had come to dominate the playing of the game, yet the amateur regulations of the RFU meant that they had to sacrifice money due to taking time off work to compete on equal terms. No working class player had achieved more than Dicky, yet even his status was not enough to allow him to pursue his sport without jeopardising his livelihood.

It was the refusal of the rugby union authorities to compromise on this issue which led in August 1895 to English rugby splitting in two and the formation of the Northern Union.

Unsurprisingly, given his treatment at the hands of the leadership of rugby union, Dicky was quick to show his support for the new body. He quickly left Heckmondwike, who remained temporarily loyal to the RFU, to join Wakefield Trinity as their captain. He made one appearance for the Yorkshire county Northern Union representative side in 1897 but his rugby league career was beset by age and severe personal problems. In January 1897 he was declared bankrupt after accumulating debts of over £300 running his pub and was forced to sell all of his household furniture to pay off his creditors. Even so, his own difficulties did not stop him helping to organise charity fund-raising matches for the trade unions during the engineers' lock out during the same year.[13]

In November 1900, the wheel turned full circle and 'Little Dick, the World's Wonder' returned to Dewsbury to play out the final three years of his career. Over a hundred years later, viewers of the Mitchell & Kenyon collection of Edwardian Northern Union rugby films were able to see footage of him run on to field at Crown Flatt as Dewsbury prepared to take on Manningham in October 1901. Following retirement as a player he spent the rest of his years in manual jobs until on 10 November 1915, just a day before his 48th birthday, he died in Leeds Infirmary. His death occurred shortly before he was due to have a second operation for cancer, and he left a widow and four children. He was buried in Wakefield Cemetery.[14]

Although forgotten in rugby union history, Dicky's memory flickered on in rugby league, which was the continuator of the glory years of pre-1895 Yorkshire and Lancashire rugby union. Thirty-five years after Lockwood's retirement, one rugby league writer recalled 'Dicky Lockwood's Deadly Tackle - once felt, never forgotten', while over a century after his birth, Eddie Waring was to regret the fact that he could not include him in *The Great Ones*.

The virtual disappearance of Dicky Lockwood's name from the annals of English rugby serves as a warning that sportsmen and women are not simply remembered for their achievements on the field of play. Their survival in the folk memory of sport is dependent on the role they can play in the creation of a mythic past. Thus Arthur Gould's name lives on in Welsh rugby union because he seemed to embody the spirit of the emerging Welsh national identity of the turn of the century. Likewise, Adrian Stoop was the personification of the dashing Edwardian English public school hero and the idealisation of everything the RFU stood for. Dicky, in contrast, could play no such role.

Indeed, to the supporters of the RFU he represented everything they wanted to forget: the virtual eclipse of middle class players by Northern manual workers in the 1890s, the rise of professionalism and the near loss of control of a sport they viewed as being uniquely theirs. Even the fact that he was a fleet-footed three-quarter seemed an affront to official rugby union history - insofar as it was spoken about at all, the Northern game before the split was thought to be so dominant because of its hardworking forwards, horny-handed sons of toil who were happy to carry out the donkey work while public school-educated backs used superior intelligence to fashion brilliant tries.

It is high time that Dicky Lockwood was restored to his rightful position as one of the greatest English players of either rugby game.

His achievements rank among the most outstanding of any age. Yet his excision from history also serves to remind us that sport is no less subject to political and social prejudice than any other form of human activity. For those who assume that sport stands above society and that excellence inevitably brings it own rewards, the career of Richard Evison Lockwood is powerful evidence to the contrary.

Notes

[1] This chapter is previously unpublished and based on a paper presented to a Sporting Heritage conference at Twickenham in 1998. Eddie Waring, *The Great Ones*, London, 1969, p. 122.

[2] *Yorkshire Post*, 10 January 1887, 18 February 1889, 9 February 1891, 4 January and 7 March 1892.

[3] *Yorkshire Post*, 10 January 1887.

[4] *The Yorkshireman*, 3 February 1887.

[5] *The Yorkshireman*, 27 November 1889.

[6] This was confirmed some years later by former Leeds Grammar School and Heckmondwike player Aulay MacAulay in the *Yorkshire Evening Post*, 9 March 1901.

[7] *Yorkshire Post*, 20 and 28 December 1890.

[8] *The Yorkshireman*, 11 November 1891.

[9] For the development of the four three-quarter system in Wales see Gareth Williams and David Smith, *Fields of Praise*, Cardiff, 1980, p. 61. For England see Tony Collins, *A Social History of English Rugby Union*, Abingdon, 2009, pp. 137-40. Stadden and McCutcheon's stories can be found in the *Athletic News*, 23 April 1906 and the *Yorkshireman*, 3 March 1887.

[10] *Yorkshire Post*, 8 January 1894. *Liverpool Mercury*, 8 January 1894.

[11] *Yorkshire Post*, 6 February 1894.

[12] *Yorkshire Chat*, 21 October 1899.

[13] *Yorkshire Post*, 7 January 1897.

[14] *Yorkshire Post*, 11 and 15 November 1915.

'A question of expediency' - Arthur Gould

3

Myth & Reality in the 1895 Rugby Spilt

Signs, symbols and artefacts play a central role in the creation and development of all sporting cultures, traditions and myths.

Yet few artefacts have acquired such a comprehensive mythology around them as William Wollen's painting 'The Roses Match', a work based on the 1893 Yorkshire v Lancashire rugby match at Bradford's Park Avenue ground.

The original hangs at Twickenham and a reproduction of it takes pride of place in the club house of Otley RUFC. It is famous - or notorious, depending on your point of view - because those players who later joined the Northern Union have been painted out.

If you look at the painting closely - and it is reproduced in the photo section of this book - it is possible to see the ghostly apparition of a player who turned professional and was subsequently painted over by the artist. It is also believed that there are other areas which have been changed to render future rugby league players 'unpersons'.

In the same way that Stalin airbrushed Trotsky out of Soviet history, so too did the rugby union conspire to repaint the history of the rugby games.[1]

Unfortunately, this neat and evocative story isn't true.

It is, however, widely believed to be true, having been retold in both rugby league and rugby union folklore, reprinted in magazines and screened on TV. In November 1994 BBC North even screened a documentary in which someone was seen pointing to where the defecting players had supposedly been painted out![2]

In fact, the painting was completed *before* rugby's split took place and was widely exhibited in Lancashire and Yorkshire in the autumn of 1895, just a couple of months after the split - when missing players would have been spotted immediately. More to the point, if Wollen had chosen to paint out all those players who joined the Northern Union he would have probably been left with two players on the field.

The split literally decimated the ranks of northern rugby union. Five years before the schism there were about 240 clubs affiliated to the RFU in Lancashire and Yorkshire. Five years after, there were about 22. Indeed by 1904, the Northern Union probably had more adult clubs affiliated to it than the RFU.[3] Almost to a man, the leading rugby players in Lancashire and Yorkshire joined the Northern Union, most with undisguised enthusiasm.

The story surrounding the Wollen painting is not the only myth about the 1895 split. One of the most well-worn is the claim that many of the northern delegates who set out for the 1893 RFU meeting to vote on broken-time payments did not arrive because they 'got lost in the metropolis, as country bumpkins used to do even in those days,' as the RFU's official *Centenary History* sneeringly asserts.[4]

Of course there is not a single piece of evidence for this,

despite the huge amount of detailed coverage of the meeting in contemporary newspapers. In truth, the supporters of broken-time lost because of the huge numbers of delegates from schools and Oxbridge delegates that had been marshaled to vote against broken-time.

A variation of this myth is retold by Morley rugby union club which believes that it was invited to send two delegates to the 1895 meeting at the George Hotel but that its representatives got drunk on the way to catch the train and failed to get to Huddersfield. The truth is that Morley were not invited (they were not viewed as a top-flight club) but that the club did join the Northern Union in May 1897 when a majority voted to join the Northern Union. Two months later supporters of the RFU founded a new club, 'Morley English Rugby Football Club', to which the present club owes its origins.[5]

Even Otley rugby union club, in whose clubhouse a copy of the Wollen painting hangs, has its own minor mythology. Although it claims to have been founded in 1865, the original Otley rugby club left the RFU in 1900 to join the Northern Union and played rugby league for six seasons before disbanding due to financial problems. The current Otley club was founded as a rugby union club only in 1907.

For rugby union, these myths symbolise its self-confidence and institutional power over the league game. For league, the myth is believed because it fits with the pattern of discrimination by union against rugby league.

And the Wollen painting myth also serves a broader purpose. It downplays the importance of the 1895 split, portraying it as a minor episode in the history of rugby union - after all, so the legend goes, it was only a few players who were painted out - rather than the devastating event which it was in reality. In fact, as we can see today by the contortions over the arrival of professionalism in union,

1895 was the defining moment, not only of rugby league, but also of rugby union. It codified amateurism as an ideology for a century and defined rugby union in England as an overwhelmingly middle class sport.

The Wollen painting therefore symbolises the three key myths which shroud the events of 1895: the myth of amateurism, the myth of the North/South divide and the myth of the northern businessman, all of which serve to obscure the true nature and meaning of the rugby's great schism.

1. The myth of amateurism

Historians of rugby have generally taken the RFU's claims to amateurism as good coin. In fact the RFU and its supporters did not necessarily object to players receiving money for playing the game - the key question was which players were receiving money?

The growth of amateur ideology in rugby dates from precisely the same period in which working class players started to make their influence felt in the 1870s and 1880s. Contrary to popular belief, the RFU itself had no rules on amateurism or professionalism until 1886. The earliest strictures against professionalism came from the Yorkshire committee in 1879, when, in response to the influx of working class players and their expectations of payment following the start of the Yorkshire Cup in 1877, they adopted from cricket the MCC's regulations on amateurism. These rules made it clear that a 'gentleman' who found himself out of pocket could legitimately claim expenses.

This contrasted sharply to the general attitude to working class players, about whom it was said, by Harry Garnett, a key leader of Yorkshire rugby, 'if they cannot afford to play, they should go without the game'.[6]

The most famous example of this double standard was Andrew Stoddart, England captain at both rugby and cricket, who went on Shaw and Shrewsbury's rugby tour of Australasia in 1888 for a payment of not less than £200.[7] On a smaller scale William Bromet, Oxford University and Yorkshire, claimed £6/13s in expenses for playing in a county game at Yorkshire in 1895.[8] Visits by southern sides to the north were taken as opportunities for indulgence by their players - Blackheath were paid almost £4 per player in expenses by Bradford for game in 1887.[9] (Incidentally the Corinthians, the very embodiment of pristine amateurism and members of the RFU, charged opponents £150 a match.)

Nor were the purveyors of the amateur ethic above 'poaching' players from other clubs, a practice which, when carried out in the North, was condemned by the RFU leadership as almost being on a par with devil worship. The Middlesex county side miraculously drew on players throughout the British Isles for important matches and Blackheath's thirst for expenses was matched only by their appetite for other club's players. In 1890 alone, they signed players from Harlequins, Clapham Rovers, Marlborough Nomads and Old Cheltonians.

This is not to suggest that amateurism was merely a cynical manoeuvre. Many in rugby union sincerely believed in its principles. Yet when push came to shove, those who upheld amateurism were prepared to compromise their principles when faced with the need to be pragmatic about fellow members of their class.

For example, the RFU took no action whatsoever against the returning 1888 tourists, despite publicly available evidence that they were being paid, in order to protect Stoddart. Likewise, in the Arthur Gould case in 1896 and 1897, when the Welsh captain was the recipient of a handsome testimonial from his supporters, and thus a professional in the eyes of the RFU, the Rugby Union ultimately compromised because, in the words of its secretary Rowland Hill, it 'was a question of expediency'.[10] Similar compromises were made during investigations into professionalism in the Midlands in the 1900s, resulting in the resignation of the RFU president Arnold Crane in 1909.

For the RFU it was not payments to players which were at issue, but payments to working class players. 'Amateurism' as a concept developed as the ideological expression of middle class attempts to subordinate working class players to their leadership.

2. The myth of the North/South divide

Traditional mythology has made the north/south divide central to the split. But although regional rivalries and organisational jealousies had been apparent in the game from at least the late 1870s, until 1888 all sections of rugby, whether in the North or the South, were united in support of amateurism.

Indeed, it was Yorkshire which introduced the first amateurism rules in 1879. It was Yorkshire and Lancashire representatives which formed the majority of the committee which drew up the RFU's first amateurism rules in 1886. It was the Yorkshire committee which hunted down 'veiled professionals' - as players who received 'under the counter' payments were known - in the game from 1886 to 1893. It was the Yorkshire committee which attacked the RFU leadership for its lack of zeal in not banning the 1888 Shaw and Shrewsbury tourists for professionalism. And it was the Yorkshire committee which attacked the Lancastrians for being soft on professionalism in 1890.

The leaders of Lancashire rugby were similarly virulent in their opposition to professionalism. The Lancashire committee refused to start a knock-out cup competition for fear of encouraging professionalism. And it was they who precipitated the final battle of rugby's civil war in 1894, by suspending Leigh, Salford and Wigan for professionalism, which led directly to the split in the following year.

This should not be surprising. The leadership of northern rugby was first and foremost drawn from men who were part of the national ruling classes. In Lancashire the Liverpool/Manchester axis which led the game was firmly based on former pupils of Rugby and Cheltenham, and to a lesser extent Eton and Harrow. The original leadership of Yorkshire rugby had been based on players educated at southern public schools.

Even those who had attended public schools in the north, such as Leeds Grammar School, Manchester Grammar School, St. Peter's in York or West Yorkshire's Bramham College, had been educated firmly in the traditions of Rugby School headmaster Matthew Arnold, and many of them, such as Lancashire's J.H. Payne or Yorkshire's W.E. Bromet, had completed their education at Oxford or Cambridge universities.

These men represented the northern bourgeoisie par excellence, coming from families which had made their money from industry, particularly textiles, or mercantile capital. The backgrounds of three of the northern presidents of the RFU, and most determined fighters against professionalism, were impeccably industrial: H.W.T. Garnett of Yorkshire was a paper manufacturer, William Cail of Northumberland was manager of a chemical works and J.W.H. Thorp of Cheshire was a textile manufacturer. But while they may have delighted in their northern roots, they unequivocally shared the instincts, aspirations and philosophies of their colleagues living in the south.

In fact, 1895 was a split *within* northern rugby. Not

simply between exclusively middle class clubs and open clubs but also within clubs: Castleford, Morley, Dewsbury to name three. Many other clubs that joined the Northern Union lost key administrators and players. The battle in rugby was therefore based not on geographical lines but on class lines, focused on differing attitudes towards working class players.

This truth of this can also be seen in the fact that during the same period trials of players for professionalism took place in virtually every area where rugby had a mass working class base - in the South West, the Midlands and South Wales.

In the south west of England, Gloucester and clubs in Torquay were investigated in the 1890s and found guilty of violations of the amateur regulations. In the Midlands, there were investigations into payments for play throughout the 1900s involving the Leicester and Coventry clubs, one of which resulted in the aforementioned resignation of RFU president Arnold Crane in 1909 after he called for expulsion of the miscreants. Clubs in the Scottish borders, where working class players were in the majority, were suspected but never convicted of being more than generous with expenses payments to players. And of course, Welsh rugby union was plagued with accusations of professionalism for almost as long as Lancashire and Yorkshire, eventually managing to partially suppress the contradiction between amateur ideal and semi-professional reality by covertly legitimising informal payments to players. But the situation in the North of England differed because of the sheer scale of working class involvement.

The reason why the split centred on Lancashire and Yorkshire was because of the huge numbers of working-class players in the region and the impossibility of controlling payments.

These problems were perceived by the RFU as being a direct threat to their control of the game. The rapidity with which soccer had become dominated by the working class player following the FA's legalisation of professionalism was not a path down which the RFU and its supporters wished to follow.

3. The myth of the northern businessman

The third myth I want to consider is that of the motor force of the split itself.

The dominant view is that the businessmen who led rugby in the North were fundamentally different from the leadership of the RFU and sought to split because of their relative autonomy and self-confidence.[11] The opposite is the case. It was the RFU and its supporters which took a decision to drive out those clubs who supported payments for play - the northern clubs would have preferred to stay.

It was working class players who brought payment for play into the sport. Up until 1888 the northern businessman had no quarrel with the amateur regulations because these did not necessarily clash with business exigencies - in fact they helped to suppress the threat of wage inflation which hit soccer in 1890s. It was only when the reality of clubs and players being banned for violations of the amateur regulations began to bite - with lucrative fixtures being cancelled and star players being banned - that some northern clubs called for broken-time payments.

The initial bourgeois consensus over amateurism therefore fractured when it became clear that, in order to impose amateurism, working class players had to be driven out of the game. In Lancashire and Yorkshire, this could not be done without wrecking rugby, as was pointed out in *The Yorkshireman* in 1891:

In the North the game is essentially dependent upon working men, both for its exposition and its support. It is a game by the masses for the masses. It is a cosmopolitan institution, in which all have an equal interest. ...To carry out such an abstract idea [amateurism] to its logical conclusion would be to depopularise the game and make it the selfish possession of the silver-spooned classes. Moreover, it would deprive the pastime of its ablest and most numerous exponents, who are essentially the working men of the North, and of its most enthusiastic supporters, who are undoubtedly the wage-earning classes.[12]

Given the sport's mass appeal and its importance to local civic life, this was not an option open to most leaders of the game in the north. Nevertheless, unlike soccer in 1884 when the northern sides threatened to split if professionalism wasn't recognised by the FA, the leaders of the senior rugby clubs by and large looked to compromise. Hence the call not for full professionalism but for broken-time - they believed that they could safeguard the RFU and its amateur ethos by opposing open professionalism.

It was only when the RFU announced that it would introduce anti-professional laws so draconian that there was no possibility of compromise that the leading northern clubs decided they had no choice but to split. Thus the Northern Union came into being as a defensive measure against the intransigent forces of middle class amateur exclusivity. Even after the split, in the 1900s, hopes were expressed by many in the NU that some form of rapprochement would take place with the RFU - in 1905 Hull proposed that the

Northern Union seek unification talks with the RFU and in 1907 Bradford actually voted to rejoin the RFU.[13]

The northern bourgeois leadership of the game itself split in 1895 over the question of their attitude to working class players. For example, textiles manufacturers could be found equally on both sides. To a certain extent this mirrored the split between the Conservative Party and the Liberal Party - without wishing to draw hard distinctions, it is the case that those supporting the Northern Union who were political tended to be Liberals, such as Harry Waller, the first NU president, and those who were opposed tended to be Conservatives, such as Baron Kilner of Wakefield.

Crudely summarised, the split in the leadership of northern rugby was between those who sought to bring some of the 'equal rights' of the free market place to rugby and those who sought to preserve a system of patronage and rigid class stratification. It was only the intransigence of the latter which forced the former to break away.

In fact, within ten years of the split, many of the industrial factory owners associated with Northern Union clubs left the game.

This haemorrhage meant that the leadership of the game largely fell into the hands of the more marginal elements of the northern middle classes - shop keepers, salesmen, music hall promoters and local government officials. The cross-class nature of rugby crowds in the 1880s disappeared too, as spectators became almost exclusively proletarian. This was repeated on the pitch - in contrast to rugby union in the region, no Cambridge University or Oxford University man ever played representative Northern Union or rugby league football. Unlike rugby union, the Northern Union became a sport virtually entirely played and watched by the working class.

Just as the myths surrounding the Wollen painting have

became accepted as facts, so too have the partial and often misleading explanations for the split.

These explanations - amateur versus professional, North versus South, sport versus business - have also served to marginalise the importance of the split and to lock rugby league out of the mainstream of British sport by presenting it as an aberration. The real cause of the 1895 split was the coming of the working class player to rugby in the 1870s and 1880s and the reluctance of the middle class leadership of rugby union to allow his participation in the sport on an equal footing. The debate in the game which preceded the split reflected the differing attitudes adopted to the working class by the middle class leaders of the game. In this, rugby echoed the debate in late Victorian society as a whole about what attitude to take towards an increasingly self-confident and assertive working class.

Notes

[1] The original version of this chapter appeared in *The Sports Historian*, No. 16, May 1996, pp. 19-27. A very useful 'Comment' on the paper by Piers Morgan was printed in the subsequent issue, No. 17, part 1, May 1997, pp. 112-3.

[2] Just a few weeks after this paper was given in 1995, the *Yorkshire Post* (26 August 1995) reproduced the Wollen painting over an article by history lecturer Gary Firth. The painting's caption solemnly proclaimed that 'the faces of those players who turned professional were masked out, leaving only the true amateurs in view'.

[3] Details of rugby union membership are taken from the *Yorkshire Post* for the appropriate years. For the 1904 comparison, see the *Northern Union Official Guide 1904/05*, Manchester, 1904, and O.L. Owen, *The History of the RFU*, London, 1955.

[4] U.A. Titley and R. McWhirter, *Centenary History of the RFU*, London, 1971, p. 113.

[5] http://www.morleyrfc.co.uk/the_history.htm. For the real history of Morley rugby see Eric Farr, 'A History of Morley Northern', *Code 13*, issue 13, 1989, pp. 45-51.

[6] H.W.T. Garnett speaking at the October 1886 RFU annual general meeting.

[7] See the correspondence of Arthur Shrewsbury for more details. This is kept at Nottinghamshire CCC HQ at Trent Bridge.

[8] *Yorkshire Owl* 18 November 1895.

[9] See my 'Noa Mutton, Noa Laaking, The origins of payment for play in rugby football' in *International Journal of the History of Sport*, vol. 12, no. 1 (April 1995), pp. 33-50.

[10] G. Rowland Hill speaking at the 1897 RFU annual general meeting.

[11] For example, see Eric Dunning and Kenneth Sheard, *Barbarians, Gentlemen and Players* (New York: New York University Press, 1979), p. 199, and Gareth Williams, 'Rugby Union' in Tony Mason (ed.) *Sport in Britain: a social history* Cambridge, 1989, p. 313.

[12] *The Yorkshireman Football Number* March 1891.

[13] The vote was eventually overturned in favour of a switch to association football, the club joining the Southern League later that year.

'The Rugby Rumpus' -
A newspaper cartoon depicts the Reverend Frank Marshall

4

Three Who Made the Rugby Revolution

Every great drama has three key characters. The hero, the villain and the traitor, the one supports the cause only to betray it later. The rugby split of 1895 is no exception to this rule.

The unfolding of the split took place over more than a decade and consumed the lives of numerous rugby officials. To many in the game, it seemed that professionalism was the inevitable next step in the evolution of rugby. In 1893 the *Yorkshire Post* journalist A.W. Pullin wrote a science fiction-style article looking back from 1918, in which he described the triumph of professional rugby around the country.

But for others, the prospect of payments for play filled them with dread. 'If the working man cannot afford to play, he must do as other people have to do who want things they cannot afford - do without', declared one writer in the *Salford Reporter* in 1894.

The events that led up to the creation of the Northern Union in 1895 were traumatic and deep-seated, as much about political and social issues as they were about rugby. In this atmosphere, personalities came to the fore who seemed to embody the ideas that caused the conflict. And for some, the dispute was to be the defining feature of their lives.[1]

Frank Marshall's Missionary Zeal

One of those who was filled with dread at the prospect of professional rugby was the Reverend Frank Marshall, the undisputed villain of rugby's drama, at least according to those who formed the Northern Union. The headmaster of King James' Grammar School in Almondbury near Huddersfield, Frank Marshall was the embodiment of the late nineteenth century quest for the purity of amateur ideals in rugby.

Marshall was not a northerner but had been born in 1845 in West Bromwich, the son of a school master. In 1868 he gained a first-class honours degree in Maths from St. John's College, Cambridge University. The following year he was ordained as a minister in the Church of England. His teaching career began as the vice-principal at Carmarthen Training College in Wales and then moved back to his native West Midlands where he was headmaster of Wednesbury Collegiate School in the West Midlands. In 1878 he was appointed head of King James' Grammar School in Almondbury, then a small private school for boys, where his career as a rugby official began.

Although he had played rugby as a schoolboy it seems that it was only when he took up the headmastership at Almondbury that he became seriously involved in the game. It is safe to assume that this was because his move to Yorkshire coincided with the start of the great rugby boom that was to engulf the county in the 1880s. The start of the Yorkshire Cup in 1877 was the catalyst for huge crowds and spurred the formation of hundreds of rugby clubs. As someone who believed in Muscular Christianity, the philosophy of *Tom Brown's Schooldays* that urged Anglicans to take part in sport to fight for their ideals, Marshall could not but help be swept up in the mania for rugby.

By the early 1880s he had become a well-respected referee, and was noted for occasionally smoking a cigar while officiating in a match. But it was following his election to the committee of the Yorkshire Rugby Union (YRU) in 1887 that he became most famous. Described as the man 'with bell, book and candle' seeking to exorcise the evil of professionalism from rugby, Marshall took it upon himself to lead the fight against payments to rugby players.

Following the RFU's introduction of its amateur regulations in 1886, any player suspected of receiving payments - whether in cash or in kind - were summoned to appear in front of the YRU committee and cross-examined as if they were in court. Those found guilty were banned from the game. Marshall helped to conduct more than twenty trials of players and clubs accused of professionalism, most famously those involving Dicky Lockwood (for a transcript of one of Marshall's cross-examinations, see the previous chapter on Dicky Lockwood). In 1890 he was elected president of the YRU.

Although Yorkshire rugby clubs were initially supportive of Marshall's attempts to purge what were known as 'veiled professionals', they soon realised that the suspension of players and clubs caused by Marshall's pursuit of amateurism were incompatible with the business of running successful teams. Teams deprived of the star players saw their crowds decline, while clubs that were suspended for paying players found their grounds closed down and were unable to pay rents or repay bank loans taken out to develop stadia.

Marshall felt that this was a small price to pay. He firmly believed that rugby's true importance was in promoting the principles of Muscular Christianity and developing the moral character of its players. Perhaps not surprisingly he also held a very patronising view of the working-class participants in the game: 'I look upon [rugby] for the working man much as I regard the same game for my boys at school'. In many ways he saw himself as a missionary taking his message to the heathens. Unfortunately for him, these values were rarely shared by their intended recipients and because of his views, and his stridency in advocating them, he found himself heckled at meetings, stoned by schoolboys on his way to work and, on one occasion, jostled at his local railway station.[2]

Given the problems that the pursuit of amateurism were causing, in the late 1880s most clubs in Yorkshire had come around to the idea of paying players money to compensate them for taking time off to play rugby, which became known as broken-time payments. Although broken-time was presented as a halfway house between amateurism and complete professionalism, Marshall refused to support the idea and he became increasingly alienated from the leadership of the game in Yorkshire. In the words of future RFU president George Berney, 'Marshall had never wavered. Almost alone, and in enemy country, he continued to hit out left and right.' In 1891 he even proposed that players suspected of receiving money to transfer to a new club should be suspended until they could prove their innocence, reversing the legal principle that the accused is innocent until proven guilty.[3]

In the midst of this struggle he found time to write and edit the first major history of rugby, *Football - The Rugby Union Game*.[4] First published in 1892, it quickly became regarded as the definitive work on the development of rugby in the nineteenth century, combining both Marshall's own work and contributions from many of the game's leading players and administrators. A book that is still worth reading today, it was a conscious attempt to prove that rugby was a creation of the public schools and that middle-class players and officials were responsible for its evolution and innovations. However, despite a chapter on the game's origins at Rugby School, there is not a single mention of William Webb Ellis.

In 1893 the leading Yorkshire clubs proposed to that year's annual general meeting of the RFU that broken-time payments should be legalised. Marshall was one of the key speakers against. He claimed that broken-time was a ruse to allow clubs to pay and therefore professionalism, adding that those who supported it should leave the RFU and form their own organisation. He was loudly heckled by Wakefield secretary J.H. Fallas, who accused him of hypocrisy. Even so, Marshall got his way and the proposal to legalise broken-time was voted down.

By now Marshall seemed to take delight in antagonising northern rugby clubs and relations between him and other officials had completely broken down. The nadir was reached in the autumn of 1893 when Marshall accused his own club - he was a committee member of Huddersfield - of paying money to George Boak and John Forsyth for them to come down from Cumberland to play at Fartown. An RFU investigation followed and Huddersfield were suspended for the rest of the year.

This was the final straw and Marshall played no further role in northern rugby. A few months after the split in rugby which he had both encouraged and played no small role in precipitating, he left Almondbury and became rector of Mileham church in Norfolk. He died there ten years later. If he was remembered as a villain by the vast majority of rugby supporters in the north, he was regarded as a hero by loyal rugby union followers. In the 1971 official centenary history of the RFU he was acclaimed as 'one of the game's immortals' and in 2008 he was nominated, although not elected, for inclusion in rugby union's International Rugby Board Hall of Fame.

James Miller's Money Troubles

If Frank Marshall was the villain of the 1895 split, James Miller would have been the candidate for rugby's hero in the early 1890s. He became the spokesman for the reformers, not only arguing for broken-time payments but also for a thirteen-a-side game. But the stormy turbulence of rugby in the mid-1890s caused psychological turmoil for many of those involved, and James Miller ended his days very far from the place where he had established his reputation.

Unlike Frank Marshall, James Arthur Miller was both a Yorkshireman and a distinguished rugby player. He was born on 19 January 1855 in Leeds, the son of an engineer. He first played rugby in the 1870s as a pupil at Leeds Middle Class School, a Church of England school which unusually for the time specialised in science and technology. He later returned as the school's science master - teaching 'magnetism and electricity' - a role in which he enjoyed great popularity with his pupils.

He played rugby as a forward for Leeds St. John's, the forerunner of Leeds RLFC, and was good enough to be selected five times for Yorkshire between 1879 and 1881. But it was an administrator of the game where he really made his mark.

He became secretary of Leeds St. John's in the 1880s, was elected as the club's representative on the YRU committee and became secretary of the YRU in 1889. This was one of the most important positions in British rugby. At that time, Yorkshire had more rugby clubs than any other county in the country and was seen as the heartland of rugby's mass popularity. His elevation to YRU secretary came at a time when the divisions over broken-time were coming to the fore and Miller saw himself as a reformer who wanted to see rugby develop to its fullest potential.

In 1891, recognising that pure amateurism was unworkable in the predominantly working class environment of northern rugby, he proposed relaxing the RFU's amateur regulations to allow players to be paid for time lost at work due to playing rugby or 'broken-time'. He argued that rugby was:

> no longer the pastime of the public schools and the leisured classes alone; it has become the sport of the masses - of the wage-earning classes in our great manufacturing centres. That being so, football legislation ought not to be for the 'silver spoon' fraternity but for working men and the Union clearly cannot legislate on the same lines for the latter as they could for the former classes. It is unreasonable to expect the same 'amateurism' from the wage-earning classes as from public school men. It is unfair to expect working men to break time to play football without their being remunerated.[5]

For Miller, making broken-time payments was the perfect middle course between the amateurism of the RFU leadership and the uncontrolled professionalism of soccer. But payments for play were part of a more wide-ranging series of reforms that he argued would make rugby more attractive and to help it counter the growing popularity of soccer. His vision for the game's future helped him get elected as president of the YRU in 1892 and in the same year he outlined another visionary plan:.

> The game had now reached a period when another radical change must be considered, and that was the reduction of players from 15 to 13. By lessening the number of forwards taking part in a game, he was convinced it would be a reform which would have precedence in the immediate future and the adoption of which would bring the game nearer the perfected state. It was clear to him that the end of the 'pushing age' had been reached and instead of admiring the physique and pushing power of those giants which took part in the game in the early stages, at any rate in the future they would be able to admire the skilful and scientific play of the game. He thought the adoption of this rule would enable the game in many parts of England to maintain an equal fight with the Association game for popular favour.[6]

His thirteen-a-side proposal was not considered by the RFU and was only seriously discussed by the Northern Union, which introduced it in 1906. But the debate on broken time gripped the rugby world and came to a head at the September 1893 RFU general meeting.

At the meeting, Miller proposed the motion that 'that players be allowed compensation for bona-fide loss of time', arguing that working class players were constantly called upon to lose their wages in order to play for the game at the highest levels yet were refused recompense for the loss of time involved. But the motion was lost by 282 votes to 136, and the RFU consequently amended its constitution so allow membership only to those clubs 'entirely composed of amateurs'. A few weeks later Frank Marshall denounced Huddersfield to the RFU and the course was set for break-up of rugby.

But when the split in 1895 came Miller was to be found on the opposite side. In stark contradiction to his previous views, he led a campaign to stop Leeds joining the Northern Union. When he was massively outvoted, he resigned from the club and joined Headingley rugby union club, one of a handful of Yorkshire clubs that remained loyal to the RFU, where he was elected chairman. He became one of the most unyielding opponents of the NU and was fanatical about maintaining the RFU's ban on any NU player being allowed to play rugby union. In 1904 he declared that 'experience had taught him that the best interests of rugby union coincided with the strictest amateurism'.

Why did rugby's most radical reformer become one of its arch-conservatives? History is littered with old men who became the enemies of their younger selves. Miller may have valued his position as an RFU administrator more than his principles. He also knew full well that the RFU would ostracise and demonise the new rugby organisation; the mutineers would not have a comfortable ride. And, of course, there is a big difference between being a loyal critic and an external opponent. He was not alone in abandoning his ideals. His co-sponsor of the broken-time proposal, Dewsbury's Mark Newsome, became president of the RFU in 1902 and A.W. Pullin, the *Yorkshire Post*'s cricket and rugby correspondent, also turned from an enthusiastic supporter of professionalism to a bitter opponent of the NU.

Miller became a stalwart of Yorkshire rugby union for the next three decades. He served on the YRU committee and was appointed its treasurer in 1922. He also survived personal tragedy, almost losing his life following a huge explosion at Roundhay Park in Leeds in 1910 which caused him to have a leg amputated.

And from there his life should have gradually trickled away, perhaps occasionally troubled by his abrupt change of mind in 1895. But there was one final act in his personal drama. For the man who had made his name by arguing that players should receive cash for their rugby talents was to be touched by the question of money for one final time.

In June 1927, at the age of seventy-two, James Miller was sentenced to six months' imprisonment for embezzlement. He had used his position as secretary to steal more than £1,000 from the Yorkshire Rugby Union over the years. He died, almost completely unnoticed and unmourned, on 10 March 1939, and was buried at Lawnswood Cemetery in North Leeds three days later. The man who life had been shaped by money left just £27.[7]

Harry Waller's New World

It is easy to identify the villain and the traitor in the dramatis personae of rugby's great split. But finding a hero is more difficult.

Up until the final few weeks, the split was not planned or prepared. Almost all the founders of the Northern Union would have preferred to compromise with the RFU and keep rugby united but reformed. But the RFU refused to make any concessions and launched a vicious war on the NU. In such circumstances the leaders of the NU were men who were pragmatic but steadfast. And foremost among them was Henry Hirst 'Harry' Waller, the man who chaired the historic meeting at the George Hotel on 29 August 1895 and was elected the founding president of the NU.

Harry Waller was born in 1861, the elder of two sons of

one of Brighouse's leading textiles manufacturers - his grandfather had introduced cotton-spinning to the town in the early nineteenth century. He attended Silcoates Grammar School near Wakefield and in 1878, falling victim to the rugby fever that was sweeping Yorkshire, he helped to found the local rugby club, Brighouse Rangers. The side soon established a reputation for itself and in 1892 Rangers were one of the founding clubs in the Yorkshire Senior Competition, the first-ever league competition in the county that comprised, as the name implied, the leading sides in the region. In April 1895 the club recorded its greatest ever triumph, when it defeated Morley 16-4 in the final of the Yorkshire Cup at Headingley.

But Harry's playing career had ended the year before after he broke four ribs in a match against Wakefield Trinity. From then on, he became a leading campaigner for a relaxation of rugby's amateur rules and for paying working class players broken-time money. An articulate public speaker, he had already made his mark in Yorkshire rugby by being a keen campaigner for league competitions and arguing for neutral 'umpires', as referees were then known.

Perhaps due to his political convictions, he quickly took a central role in the campaign for broken time. A lifelong Liberal who always remembered being introduced to the radical John Bright as a child, he became the Liberal chairman of Greetland Urban District Council in 1905, was the founding senior vice-chairman of Urban District Councils' Association and in 1906 was appointed a Justice of the Peace. His political principles guided his philosophy of rugby, believing that 'the working man player should not be penalised by losing wages for playing football'.

In November 1894 he was chairman of the first meeting of the leading Yorkshire and Lancashire clubs, which had been called to organise combined opposition to the RFU's increasing victimisation of senior northern clubs. By that time it was becoming clear to all that the RFU was preparing to drive the northern clubs out. Up until that point there had been a great deal of mutual suspicion between the two counties, but under Waller's chairmanship the most powerful counties in English rugby now spoke with one voice.

It was therefore no surprise that he was the chairman of the most historic meeting in the history of rugby that took place on 29 August 1895 at Huddersfield's George Hotel.

The first decision of the new Northern Union was to legalise payments of no more than six shillings per day for broken time. Waller later explained that this reform was necessary to save the game: 'rugby football in the North - for every part of the Kingdom in fact where there was a preponderance of working class players - could not be honestly carried out under the existing by-laws of the English Union'. At the meeting Waller was elected president, a position he was to hold for the next two years. Although not announced publicly, he also played another crucial role by acting as a guarantor to the bank for the NU.[8]

Waller played the central role in developing the NU's self-image as a democratic sport. In 1894 he described how he valued rugby because 'it was a fact that the game brought men together and united them in brotherhood which could hardly be found elsewhere'. Two years after the split he taunted those in the RFU who had predicted disaster for the rebels by quoting statistics to show that violent play was far more prevalent in rugby union than in the NU.

'Not bad for uneducated working man players', he said, throwing the stereotype back at his opponents. He did not flinch from the difficulties faced by the new organisation, but predicted in 1896 that success would come provided that 'we stick to our guns'. It did. In the two years of his presidency the NU grew from its original 22 clubs to over 150.[9]

His experiences as a paternalist employer - in 1890 he had taken over the running of the family business - motivated his belief in the importance of the social role of the NU. He saw rugby as a means of assisting working class players to better themselves, and was instrumental in introducing the 'work clauses' into the NU's rules in 1898, whereby only those in regular employment were allowed to play, arguing that 'the Northern Union was anxious to make football the means of improving the positions of players'.[10]

As president of the NU, he oversaw a number of rule changes, such as the 1897 abolition of the line-out (which he had unsuccessfully proposed a year earlier), that were to lay the basis for modern rugby league. Stepping down from the presidency in 1897, he continued to play a leading role on the NU's general committee, most notably in helping to steer the game towards professionalism. In 1902 he resigned from the general committee due to health reasons.

Although Brighouse Rangers disbanded in 1906 due to dire financial problems caused by the depression in the textiles industry which afflicted the town, Waller's involvement in the game continued through regular attendance at Halifax rugby league club's matches.

He did not waver in his support for the game he had done so much to create. In 1930 he sent a telegram to the RFL, the original of which is still kept in the RFL archives, protesting its decision to stage an unprecedented fourth Ashes Test match after the third Test had been drawn 0-0 at Swinton. Tradition had been broken and 'Mammon' had triumphed in the quest for a lucrative fourth Test, he complained.

In November 1945, as the only surviving original member of the NU committee, he was the guest of honour of the Rugby Football League at a lavish banquet to mark the fiftieth anniversary of the founding of the game.

He died aged 87 on 19 May 1949 at his home at West Vale, near Brighouse, and was buried in Brighouse Cemetery. He may not have been a hero, but when it was needed most he stood steadfast in support of the right of working-class players to play rugby without discrimination. Without him, the Northern Union would not have been the organisation it was and rugby league would be the sport it is.

Notes

[1] This chapter is based on entries I wrote for the three men for H. C. G. Matthew and Brian Harrison (eds), *The Oxford Dictionary of National Biography*, Oxford 2004, available online at www. oxforddnb.com.

[2] Marshall 'Payment for Broken Time at Rugby football',
Athletic News Football Annual 1892, Manchester, 1893, p. 149.

[3] G.F. Berney in Revd Frank Marshall and Leonard Tosswill (eds),
Football - The Rugby Union Game, 2nd Edition, London, 1925, p. 57.

[4] The book is now available online at
www.archive.org/details/footballrugbyuni00marsrich

[5] *The Yorkshireman Football Number,* March 1891.

[6] *Yorkshire Post*, 9 October 1892.

[7] *Yorkshire Evening Post*, 4 October 1927 and 11 March 1939.

[8] *Yorkshire Post*, 29 April 1896.

[9] *Yorkshire Post*, 30 April 1894 and 22 April 1897.

[10] *Yorkshire Post*, 23 May 1898.

5

The Curious Rise & Fall
of Leeds Parish Church

On 7 April 1900, 20,000 people packed into the Clarence Road ground in the centre of Leeds to watch the city's leading rugby league team earn a hard fought 5-5 draw with Runcorn in the quarter-final of the Northern Union Challenge Cup.

The club was not Leeds. Nor was it Hunslet. It was Leeds Parish Church, Yorkshire rugby union champions in 1896, a top three Yorkshire Northern Union club in 1899 and Challenge Cup semi-finalists in 1900.

But despite it on-field success and off-field popularity just fifteen months later, the club was dead, killed off by the very people who brought it into existence a quarter of a century previously.

However, this isn't just another story about a defunct rugby club of long ago. Many other famous football and rugby sides have their roots in church teams: Aston Villa and Wakefield Trinity for example. But the curious life and death of Leeds Parish Church is possibly the best example of the failure of the Church of England's attempts to bring Muscular Christianity to the working classes in the late nineteenth century.[1]

Muscular Christianity was based on the belief that physical activity played a crucial role in developing Christian gentlemen, by teaching courage, self-reliance and manly character through the playing of sport. The classic text of this philosophy was Thomas Hughes' fictional account of life at Rugby School, *Tom Brown's Schooldays*. The growth of Muscular Christianity broadly coincided with a growing concern in the Church of England that it was losing contact with urban working classes. Many in the church felt that they needed to understand and participate in popular culture to bring Christianity to the masses. Much of this activity was known as 'rational recreation', as its proponents sought to bring uplifting morality to working class leisure activities. Rugby provided the perfect vehicle for the combination of Muscular Christian philosophy and Anglican evangelism: as the Reverend Frank Marshall, probably the most famous clergyman in the game, put it 'I believe in the value of [Rugby] in developing the physique, in influencing the character, and in improving the moral as well as the physical well being of the working man player'.[2]

Muscular Christianity's attempts to reach out to the working classes were generally carried out through the provision of Sunday schools, Bible classes and Young Men's Societies.[3] The Leeds Parish Church rugby club was founded in March 1874 by the Reverend E.H .Dykes, who had played rugby as a public schoolboy at Durham, from the church's A Division Bible Class recreation club - which also included athletics, cricket and draughts sections. Based at the heart of Leeds's most impoverished inner city area, the club was described by the journalist A.W. Pullin, writing in the *Athletic News*, as 'the embodiment of that sane doctrine of

Muscular Christianity'.[4] Its commitment to Muscular Christianity can be gauged by a sermon of 1879, in which the Reverend Maurice Ponsonby reminded his congregation not to forget

> the influence which bodily exercise, such as manly games and sports, has upon the character; these often develop a character as much as books, and when the young are engaged in them they are preserved from idleness, which is the root of much evil. England perhaps owes more than any county to its noble games ... Some people seem to think that a religious life cannot go hand in hand with a life of amusement [but] the very fact of being good at games may be more of an assistance to their lives for God.[5]

The club grew slowly at first and it wasn't until the start of the 1880s that it began to be seen as serious force in the game.

In 1879 its Clarence Road ground was fenced in, indicating that significant numbers of people were now watching its games. At the start of the 1884-5 season, the club - now nicknamed as 'T' Lads Ower T' Bridge' by its supporters - erected a grandstand which could hold a thousand people. Hand in hand with rising crowds came success on the playing field.

In 1888 the side reached the quarter finals of the Yorkshire Cup and the following year they almost defeated the touring Maori team. When league competitions began in Yorkshire rugby in 1892, Leeds Parish Church was an automatic choice for the second division, known as the Number Two Competition, and in their three years in that competition they finished fourth, first and third. The importance of the club was recognised in 1888 when its ground was chosen to stage Yorkshire's county championship match against Northumberland.

Leeds Parish Church therefore became the flagship of the Anglican church's involvement in Yorkshire rugby. Church-based rugby teams blossomed in Yorkshire in the 1880s, as churches sought to capitalise on the football boom and set up their own sides. However, the popularity of rugby among the working classes was beginning to undermine the control the churches had over their clubs and their ability to impart Christian values to their players and supporters. When the Yorkshire Church Temperance Challenge Shield was started in 1887, one of its rules was that players must be bona fide members of a church, church school or Anglican temperance society.[6] But the competition rapidly became notorious for clubs' cavalier attitude to its teetotal rules and was wracked by accusations of players being brought in from other sides - 'ringers' - and the flouting of the age limits - the competition was intended to be for players under twenty-one. In 1888 it was forced to revise its rules to bar clubs which had pubs as team headquarters, but even this didn't stop Hull Britannia from proudly displaying the trophy in a Hull pub after a famous victory.[7]

Most church-based clubs initially allowed only those who actually went to church to play for their teams but most soon found themselves having to compromise and allow outsiders to play if they wished to stay competitive. Indeed, it was not unusual for churchmen, after having formed a football club, to lose their enthusiasm for the game when faced with the less than Corinthian zealotry of their working class recruits, as a Bradford curate discovered after forming a youth side and suffering 'complaints and reproaches from the mothers of his protégés about black eyes, sore bones and all the other luxuries accompanying the game. He was so intimidated that he now wants to back out, but these exuberant youths, having tasted the sweets of victory, insist on going on'.[8] As working class players and spectators continued to flock into the game, it seems that the church name was little more than a flag of convenience for many clubs, with only minimal involvement from the clergy, as Peter Bailey's study of leisure in Bolton during the same period also showed.[9] This was admitted by Nether Green Sunday School in Leeds after an inquiry into allegations that their team had deliberately set out to injure an opponent during a match against the Leeds Good Shepherd side:

> We have not kept a sufficiently close connection with and oversight of the football club which uses the name of the school. Matters have been left too much to the management of the players themselves, with the result that, contrary to the original intention of the officers of the school, the team is largely composed of those who have no connection with it. We feel that it would be incumbent on us to re-organise the club and bring it under more immediate control.[10]

Unfortunately for Muscular Christianity's adherents, Leeds Parish Church was to become the most notorious of all the church clubs. In 1889 the club was investigated by the Yorkshire Rugby Union following accusations that it paid its players. In January 1890 it was suspended for two months after the inquiry found that it had altered its accounts to hide illegal gifts to players of watches, suits, cigars, champagne and oyster suppers, not to mention fixing them up with jobs, contrary to RFU rules.[11] In 1893 the club once again came under suspicion for illegally milking the Yorkshire Rugby Union (YRU) players' injury insurance fund to subsidise their own under-the-table payments to players - who had somehow managed to receive £100 more than they paid into the fund.[12] That same year the club pulled off an amazing coup when it apparently persuaded three Welsh players to 'go North' and play for them - it was only later revealed that the three had come up to play for Holbeck, a neighbouring Leeds club, who had put them up in a pub near the Church on the night they arrived in Leeds. This had come to the attention of the Church's club officials who raced round to the pub and offered the three jobs at the local Waterloo colliery on condition they play for them. When the Holbeck officials came round the next day to see their new recruits, they had disappeared, only to reappear in the Leeds Parish Church line-up the following Saturday![13]

On the field, the club gained a reputation for being one of the most violent sides in the game. In 1892 the team had undertaken a short tour of Ireland. The vigour of their play so shocked the Irish clubs that the Northern Division of the Irish RFU threatened to bring criminal charges against them after a game in Belfast, accusing the Church team of roughness, tripping, fighting and generally playing 'in a pugilistic manner;' which was 'brutal in the extreme'. Cosmo Lang, the future Archbishop of Canterbury then working as a curate at the church, was forced to appear before the YRU to answer charges of violent play.[14]

Their supporters had the same reputation for unchristian conduct. Much to the chagrin of the Church, betting was widespread on the terraces, but this was a minor problem compared to the treatment handed out to referees. Jeering, stone-throwing and general intimidation of referees was so bad that the club had great difficulty in getting officials for its home games. On one Saturday in 1890 it was claimed that no less than fifteen referees had refused to officiate in matches at their ground. This reluctance was perhaps understandable considering the send-off given to one referee after presiding over a game against Castleford which the Church lost, as *The Yorkshireman* described: 'The referee had to climb the boards [surrounding the ground], be ferried across the canal to make good his escape and the bus which he took along East Street was followed by an infuriated and howling mob uttering the most demoniacal yells'.[15]

As if to rub salt in the wounds of the increasingly demoralised Church clergy, the chances of the rugby club winning adherents to Muscular Christian principles, which were never more than very slim, turned to dust as the club was taken to the hearts of Leeds's growing Jewish immigrant community. From the early 1880s many Jewish refugees fleeing pogroms in Tsarist Russia had settled in Leeds and the proximity of the Church to the Jewish quarter of the city meant that many of them became the club's most committed and partisan spectators. Indeed, in the 1890s it was common for the Church supporters as a whole to be known by the anti-Semitic epithet 'sheenies' or worse.

After its suspension by the YRU in 1890, the clergy had tried to wrest back control of the club by trying to re-impose the original rule that only bona-fide members of the church Sunday school could play for the side, but this proved to be impossible. In fact, by the mid-1890s much of the enthusiasm shown by the clergy for rugby was beginning to wear thin. As early as 1890 the Bishop of Chester, on a pastoral visit to Leeds, chose to use the pulpit to denounce professionalism in rugby, 'even at the risk of giving offence to every working man in England'. In 1892, the Yorkshire Church Temperance Challenge Shield committee gave up the ghost and abandoned the competition. In 1893 the vicar of Farsley, near Leeds, denounced football as 'a fascination of the devil and the twin sister of the drink system'.[16] Some of this hostility was due to a residual suspicion of sports among the more puritan-minded clergy dating back to the first half of the century, but it was undeniable that many Muscular Christians had begun to seriously doubt rugby's usefulness as an agent of evangelism among the urban working classes. The exodus of men of the cloth from the game was such that, speaking at a Church Congress in Exeter in 1894, the secretary of the RFU, Rowland Hill, called on clergy to stop criticising from the sidelines and 'make their influence felt' by playing a role in the sport once more.[17]

Following the formation of the Northern Union in 1895, Leeds Parish Church initially stayed loyal to the RFU and in the season following the split won the Yorkshire league championship. But in the summer of 1896 the club voted, with just five votes against, to join the NU.[18] Continuing its success, in 1898 Leeds Parish Church finished in the top eight of the Yorkshire Senior Competition and the following year they were fourth. 1900 saw them reach the semi-finals of the Challenge Cup. Their crowds appear to have increased too - aside from the 20,000 for the 1900 cup quarter final, games against local rivals sometimes attracted over ten thousand spectators. Their fourth round tie against Batley in 1900 attracted over 15,000 people. The club finished in a higher league position than the more senior Leeds club four out of five years.

Although they seem to have lost their reputation for on-field roughness, their spectators retained the full glory of their dubious fame. In 1900 the club was fined £20 after Brighouse Rangers' Charlie Denham was struck by a one and a half inch steel nut and his team mate Eli Robinson was hit between the eyes by a heavy cinder thrown by spectators as they left the ground. A little later that year, the game against Halifax was stopped in the second half by the referee, who refused to carry on until club officials had ejected a Church supporter who was 'using filthy and abusive language'.[19]

Given such behaviour, it was unsurprising that the Reverend Sidney Gedge, an avowed exponent of Muscular Christianity, could argue in 1900 that 'the spectator is an element foreign to sport'.[20] This type of remark was not unusual from rugby union supporters but the significance of Gedge was that later in the same year he was appointed as a curate at the church. All curates were automatically made vice-presidents of the rugby club, but rarely concerned themselves with its activities. Gedge, however, was a Scottish rugby union international, a personal friend of RFU secretary Rowland Hill and an active referee. He was a key mover in the revival of Yorkshire rugby union after the split had decimated it. Originally, he had been asked to play for Leeds Parish Church but had said that it 'would not altogether have been a good thing' to play in the Northern Union. Nevertheless, this didn't stop him being involved in the financial management of the club, despite the fact that, according to rugby union rules, any involvement whatsoever with a Northern Union club was an expellable offence - but Rowland Hill had assured him that 'the rules of professionalism were not intended to apply to cases of that kind'.[21]

Although not immediately apparent, the club was now living on borrowed time. The lease on their Clarence Road ground was to expire in August 1901, but, as A.W. Pullin pointed out, Parish Church had had ample time to relocate and had even been offered a ground on the nearby York Road. Indeed, according to the *Athletic News*, they were fast becoming Leeds's 'most prominent club - judged from the standpoint of central situation and public support'.[22] However, Parish Church did nothing to find another ground - and, completely out of the blue, on 18 July Gedge chaired a special meeting of the club which decided to 'abandon Northern Union Rugby football for the present'. Within eight weeks of voting to disband in July 1901, the club's property had been auctioned off.[23] As if it were rugby's Atlantis, the club simply disappeared from the sporting map - and one does not have to be a conspiracy theorist to see the hand of rugby union supporters as one of the reasons for the club's abrupt end.

And so Leeds Parish Church rugby club returned to whence it came, laying to rest the hopes of Muscular Christians that rugby could bring middle-class morality to the masses. Despite the best efforts of the Muscular Christians, working class culture remained firmly rooted in the pub and the local community and was deeply hostile to the patronising efforts of middle class clergy to change them, as the Reverend Frank Marshall found to his cost. Leeds Parish Church's going over to the Northern Union was the final straw for the clergy. In the eyes of Muscular Christians, the NU was opposed to traditional English sporting values. This was not based solely on class prejudice towards its overwhelmingly working class players and spectators, but also on a belief that the new union undermined the importance of rugby in British national life: the NU no longer played rugby for physical training and moral development but for pounds, shillings and pence. The NU's legalisation of payment for play would, as journalist B.F. Robinson put it, force the game to 'pander to the howling mobs that crowd the circular stands of some Yorkshire coliseum'.[24]

It was this disillusionment with the failure of the working classes to respond their patronage, coupled with a deep hostility to the working classes' own view of sport, which led Sidney Gedge and his supporters to close down the Leeds Parish Church club so dramatically. In doing so, they once again demonstrated the almost unbridgeable chasm which separated the classes at the opening of the twentieth century.

Notes

[1] This chapter is based on the article 'How Muscular Christianity met its match: The curious rise and fall of Leeds Parish Church Recreation Club, 1874-1901' *Sporting Heritage*, vol. 1, no. 2, Autumn 1996, pp. 47-55. For more information on the club, see also Trevor Delaney's 'A Brief History of T' Lads Ower T' Bridge' in *Code 13*, issue 6, March 1988, pp. 11-20.

[2] Reverend Frank Marshall 'Payment for Broken Time at Rugby football' in *Athletic News Football Annual 1892*, Manchester 1893, p. 149.

[3] For more on the organised churches' relationship to the working classes, see K.S. Inglis, *The Churches and the Working Class in Victorian England*, London 1963.

[4] A.W. Pullin, the self-appointed doyen of Yorkshire cricket and football writing, was the son of a clergyman and himself a vigorous advocate of muscular Christianity. *Yorkshire Evening Post*, 9 February 1902. Details about the importance of the Leeds Parish Church itself can be found in P.S. Morrish, 'Leeds and Dismemberment of the Diocese of Ripon,' *Publications of the Thoresby Society, Miscellany*, second series volume 4, 1994.

[5] *The Leeds Parish Church Magazine*, December 1879, pp. 311-2.

[6] *Yorkshire Post*, 15 October 1887.

[7] *Yorkshire Post*, 5 December 1887 and 18 July 1888.

[8] *The Yorkshireman*, 16 February 1884.

[9] Peter Bailey, *Leisure and Class in Victorian England*, London 1978, p. 147.

[10] *Yorkshire Post* ,11 November 1893.

[11] *The Yorkshireman*, 12 February 1890

[12] *Yorkshire Post*, 9 May 1891, 4 June 1892 and 4 May 1893. *The Yorkshireman*, 14 February 1893.

[13] *Yorkshire Post*, 10 November 1891 and *The Yorkshireman*, 31 January 1893.

[14] *Yorkshire Post*, 30 September 1890 and 9 March 1892.

[15] *Yorkshire Post*, 4 November 1888. *The Yorkshireman*, 24 September 1890.

[16] *Yorkshire Post*, 22 March 1893

[17] *Clarion*, 20 October 1894

[18] *Yorkshire Post*, 20 and 21 May 1896.

[19] *Yorkshire Post*, 4 October and 3 December 1900.

[20] *Yorkshire Post*, 24 April 1900.

[21] *Yorkshire Post*, 6 December 1900.

[22] *Athletic News*, 5 August 1900.

[23] *Athletic News*, 22 July 1901. *Yorkshire Post*, 10 September 1901.

[24] B.F. Robinson, *Rugby Football*, London 1896.

'An uncivilised sport?' - Gus Risman in action

6

Seventy-One Deaths...
& Other Myths About Rugby League

There's an old saying that a lie can be halfway around the world before the truth has even got its boots on. Anyone who spends any time reading books or searching the internet about the history of rugby will soon come across one of the most outrageous examples of that remark. This particular untruth is the claim that seventy-one players were killed playing rugby in Yorkshire between 1890 and 1893 and that almost four hundred other players were seriously injured.

This is a story that is repeated not only on hastily put-together websites but also in the work of serious historians from around the world. Even Neil Hanson's excellent 1995 collection of rugby league articles, *Rugby League Masterpieces*, carries the same assertion. Not surprisingly, this evidence is used by many to demonstrate the violent nature of rugby league and of rugby in the North of England just before the 1895 split.

There's only one problem. Not a word of it is true.

1895 & All That...

The story first emerged in 1979 with the publication of Eric Dunning and Ken Sheard's book on the development of rugby, *Barbarians, Gentlemen and Players*. As we will see in the next chapter on the split between soccer and rugby, the book was based on shaky historical research. This became even more apparent when the book dealt with rugby league. Basing themselves on the theory that rugby union was an example of a 'civilising process' at work, they set out to demonstrate that rugby in the north of England before and after the 1895 split was especially violent. In doing so they managed to inflict greater violence on historical truth than even the dirtiest player could hope to mete out to his opponents.[1]

Barbarous attacks on the truth

Barbarians, Gentlemen and Players uses statistics that show seventy-one players lost their lives playing rugby in Yorkshire between 1890 and 1893, alongside another 366 unfortunate souls who broke legs, arms and collarbones, or sustained other injuries. This claim is based on a short passage that co-author Ken Sheard found in a press cutting from the *Wakefield Express* of 8 April 1893 that reads:

> The following is a table showing the number of football casualties during the season as reported in the newspapers, together with a summary of the results for the season just closing and for the two preceding seasons [it is followed by a chart that is reprinted on p. 187 of the book]

As we can see, it makes no reference to Yorkshire. Nor does it make any reference to rugby. Yet the data is introduced by Dunning and Sheard as 'some figures on the deaths and injuries incurred in Yorkshire rugby prior to the 'split' that can serve to introduce the discussion' on 'the relationship between the roughness of Northern Union football and its spectator appeal'.[2]

These figures are so flawed that they do not pass the test of serious evidence. The *Wakefield Express* copied them directly from a series of articles entitled 'The Butcher's Bill' which had appeared in W.T. Stead's London newspaper *Pall Mall Gazette* over the previous three years. Stead's newspaper was pursuing a campaign against 'the dangers of football' but the figures were widely considered to be unreliable, so much so that a disclaimer was added to the *Gazette's* 1892 article stating that 'neither we nor the author can vouch personally for the accuracy of the following statements'.[3]

The articles listed 'football accidents' across the whole of the British Isles, plus some in Australia, and included both association and rugby from schoolboy to international level. The lists were random and unsystematic - an unnamed Blackburn Rovers player 'was hurt' in a November 1891 match while a death due to peritonitis was 'caused probably by a kick on the football field.' An accident at a match in Warriston was recorded although 'the nature of which was not stated.' Unsurprisingly, the *Yorkshire Post* criticised these figures, saying that 'the list is inaccurate in more than one instance,' as did the arch opponent of working-class professionalism Scottish headmaster H.H. Almond in the magazine *Nineteenth Century*.[4]

Having been told by at least two researchers that their data was wrong, in the new 2006 edition of *Barbarians, Gentlemen and Players* Dunning and Sheard admitted that these figures were 'a serious mistake'. However, they go on to argue bizarrely that 'they were not too wide of the mark' and cite statistics that appeared in the *Lancet* in the 1890s which claim that ninety-six players were killed playing football between 1891 and 1899.[5]

In fact, the evidence presented by the *Lancet* simply compounds Dunning and Sheard's original error. As with the *Pall Mall Gazette* claims, the *Lancet* figures do not refer to rugby in Yorkshire of any code. They cover both Association and Rugby football across the country. And, like the *Pall Mall Gazette* and its original statistics, the *Lancet* itself is sceptical of their accuracy: 'we have made no special effort to obtain a complete roll of the casualties but that we have simply recorded such as we have chanced to come across in the columns of our contemporaries'.[6] And, of course, they give absolutely no support to Dunning and Sheard's claims about northern rugby.

Despite this, Dunning and Sheard go on to claim that the *Lancet* data is 'supportive' of their argument that 'in late nineteenth century Britain, football, especially the Rugby form, was viewed as a hazardous activity'.[7] But it is not supportive at all. In fact, the *Lancet* drew precisely the opposite conclusion. It argued that it was *soccer* - not rugby - that was the most dangerous of the football codes. In 1894 it devoted a major article to the subject, examining both codes in detail, and came to the conclusion that:

> it is our opinion that Association, at first sight a tame game compared with the other, is possibly more perilous than Rugby Union; and that its modern developments, though in many ways so similar, are more certainly towards danger than are the developments in the tactics of the older branch.[8]

It returned to the subject again in 1907, following the split in rugby and the massive expansion in the popularity of soccer that had taken place over the previous decade. It saw no reason to change its opinion: 'everything seems to show that the degree of danger incurred by players is greater in the dribbling than in the carrying game'.[9]

This is not just poor research. It also defies common sense. If the figure of seventy-one deaths over three seasons was true, that means that almost twenty-four players were being killed playing rugby in Yorkshire every season. This amounts to roughly one every ten days in a normal season. Dunning and Sheard obviously think that the north was such a violent place that the almost weekly deaths of rugby players would merely warrant a small paragraph in the sports pages of a local newspaper. Do they really believe that such traumatic events would go unnoticed by the press, politicians and the public? If not, where is the evidence of what would be an entirely justified public outcry?

Any sensible view of the sources provided for rugby-related deaths in Yorkshire demonstrates that Dunning and Sheard's contentions about the violence of northern rugby are not grounded in historically reliable evidence. In short, they are simply untrue.[10]

Dummy half-backs and false insurance claims

But their desire to paint rugby league as a violent game does not stop there. Dunning and Sheard go on to claim that the decisions of the first Annual General Meeting of the Northern Union 'shows that the NU authorities believed the roughness of rugby league to be one of its most problematic aspects' and that it introduced 'the half-back rule' to reduce violent play. It showed nothing of the sort.[11]

In reality, the meeting was not an AGM but a special meeting held in December 1895 to discuss rule changes, and it introduced a rule which specified that the non-feeding scrum-half could not advance beyond the back row of his own forwards before the ball had come out of the scrum. The rule demonstrated, say Dunning and Sheard, that the game's authorities believed that 'the violence of rugby league was dysfunctional for the maintenance of spectator support'.[12]

But wait a minute. Doesn't the fact that this rule change was made to an existing RFU rule, suggest that this was an attempt by the NU to clean up *rugby union rules*, under which the new organisation was still playing?

Under rugby union scrummage rules the defending scrum-half could effectively stand next to his opposing number while waiting for the ball to emerge from the back of the scrum. Inevitably this led to a confrontations between scrum-halves, which would then often involve the back row of the forwards, making it very difficult to pass the ball away from the scrum quickly and cleanly. Although the introduction of the half-back rule did reduce opportunities for violence at the scrum, its main purpose was to open up play and allow the ball to be passed away from the scrum to the stand-off half and the three-quarters much more rapidly. Thus the primary aim was not to reduce violence in rugby league, as Dunning and Sheard claim, but to reduce the opportunities for violence and stifling play which the then current *rugby union* rules allowed. Indeed, this view is confirmed by no less an authority than William Cail, a former president of the RFU who in 1902 proposed that rugby union should adopt the rule in order to 'popularise' its game and make it more attractive in the face of threats from soccer and the NU.[13]

As to the claim that the NU authorities thought that violence in their sport was especially problematic, this is contradicted by the NU's founding president and chief spokesman, Harry Waller. Speaking after the 1897 Challenge

Cup final, he contrasted the forty-five NU players who had been reported by referees for violent play that season with the 150 reported for violence in rugby union in Yorkshire alone during the same period. To further aid the comparison he noted that the NU had 150 clubs in membership at the time, probably slightly more than the Yorkshire Rugby Union.[14]

It doesn't stop there. Determined to demonstrate the violence of league, Dunning and Sheard go on to claim to have discovered further evidence 'that rugby league remained physically dangerous' because 'in 1910, the Essex and Suffolk Insurance Company refused to continue insuring players'.[15]

As any decent insurance investigator would say, this claim has no merit. In fact, Essex and Suffolk's withdrawal of insurance had nothing to do with violence in rugby league but was a consequence of the provisions of the 1906 Workmen's Compensation Act. The act, which among other things extended compensation for injuries sustained at work to professional soccer and rugby footballers, significantly increased the potential benefits payable to employees injured at work. The small pool of professional football clubs of both codes meant that insurance companies put themselves at significant risk if faced with paying compensation out on an extensive scale, thus making them wary of underwriting football insurance. To counter the difficulties of finding affordable insurance, the Football League, along with the Southern League and the Scottish Football League, formed the Football Mutual Insurance Federation in 1907. The reluctance of the insurance companies to insure footballers was confirmed to some extent by the fact that in the 1910-11 season the FMIF made a loss of £200, leading to the Football League starting a new insurance federation in 1912.[16]

The minutes of the Northern Union meeting at which the insurance problem was discussed, which are cited in *Barbarians, Gentlemen and Players*, note the similar experiences of the soccer authorities:

> The Secretary reported that the Essex & Suffolk Insurance Company refused to continue Football Insurance, and that he could not get any of the strong offices to take it up. The question of forming a Mutual Insurance Company to take over the risks was suggested, and it was decided to leave the matter in the hands of the Emergency Committee, the Secretary in the meantime to get in touch with Mr J. Bentley [a president of the Football League and vice-president of the Football Association], with respect to the Mutual Insurance Company formed by the Association League.[17]

This is indeed what happened and a mutual insurance scheme was set up by the NU later that month. As an indication of the levels of payments made to injured players, it is worth examining how much was actually paid out in insurance claims at this time. In the three years before Essex and Suffolk stopped insuring rugby league players, total sums of £17, £12/6s and £18/8s/4d were paid to injured players, amounts which hardly suggest huge numbers of players being laid low by on-field acts of violence.[18]

Indeed, when examined properly, not a single example used by Dunning and Sheard indicates an unusually large of amount of violence in rugby league. While it is undoubtedly true that the game could be violent, there is no evidence to suggest that it was any more violent than any other code of football - indeed, the NU authorities took active steps to make it less violent than rugby union.

To put it plainly, Dunning and Sheard's assumptions are wrong, their research flawed and their knowledge of history weak at best.

Whose civilisation? Whose history?

There's an obvious problem with *Barbarians, Gentlemen and Players* when it deals with rugby league. Using their theory of the 'civilising process', it would be easy for Dunning and Sheard to argue that the NU's rule changes were part of a process of 'civilising' rugby union.

When one takes into account the move to thirteen players per side and the abolition of the dangerous rucks and mauls in favour of the more orderly play the ball after a tackle, there appears to be a very strong case in favour of the argument that the abandonment of rugby union rules and the evolution of the distinctive rugby league rules represented the creation of a more civilised form of rugby.

But they don't follow the logic of their argument. And that is because of the underlying bias at the heart of the theory of the 'civilising process'.

For supporters of this theory believe the 'civilising process' always flows downwards from the upper classes. So the predominantly working-class Northern Union form of rugby must be more violent than the more middle-class rugby union game. Indeed, *Barbarians, Gentlemen and Players* does not seriously discuss the question of violence in modern rugby union. Given the revelations about the violence in international rugby union that emerged during the 1970s when the book was written (especially the notorious 1974 British Lions tour to South Africa, in which the British side prepared the call '99' to start an all-in brawl, and the no less violent 1975 England tour of Australia), one would expect a little more serious consideration of the matter.

This one-sided view of civilisation and violence can also be seen in the short discussion on soccer hooliganism which comes at the end of the book - and which bizarrely argues that a solution to the problem was to persuade hooligans to play rugby union.

Identifying football hooligans as working class, Dunning and Sheard claim that 'such groups have been subjected to civilising pressures externally, e.g. from the higher classes and the state...'.[19] The implication that opposition to gang violence comes only from the upper classes and the state is to ignore the forces for social progress that have historically existed within working-class communities: the trade unions, political parties, tenants' organisations, co-operative societies, youth clubs and so on. Indeed for many working-class people, especially those whose skins are not white, much of the violence they experience in their daily lives comes from the state itself, in the form of the police, a supposed agency of the 'civilising process'.

When it comes to sport, it is also the case that middle-class football players of both codes were often seen by their working-class opponents as being more violent.

Certainly the famous amateur club the Corinthians played a very robust style of soccer that involved vigorous use of the shoulder charge, a feature that often unsettled their professional opponents. Jim Sullivan and Gus Risman, who both played league and union, argued that league was a cleaner and less violent form of rugby. And as historian Douglas Reid has pointed out, many of the calls to reform folk football in the first half of the nineteenth century came from working-class Methodists and Chartists.[20]

There are also dangers in accepting the claims of those

who were engaged in attempting to 'civilise' the working classes.

For example, the campaigns to ban animal-baiting and fighting sports in the early nineteenth century were usually directed almost entirely against the working class and its sports. One of the most common criticisms of the Royal Society for the Prevention of Cruelty to Animals, founded in 1824, was that it did nothing to oppose upper-class sports such as hunting and shooting – and indeed, many of the RSPCA's most prominent supporters were huntsmen. As with amateurism later in the century, 'civilised behaviour' was something that the upper classes defined for the working classes but which they did not necessarily apply to themselves.

The point, of course, is that 'civilised' is a hugely value-laden term, one which has historically been used to justify the subjugation of those deemed to be 'uncivilised' by their rulers. Those who support the sociological theory of the 'civilising process' are merely providing a sophisticated version of the idea that the working classes are unintelligent, violent and in need of guidance by those who see themselves as their betters. To put it crudely, it's like a *Daily Mail* editorial written in academic jargon.

And when it comes to rugby, the same prejudices are used to argue that union must be superior to league.

Rugby league is, in the famous words of a former Orrell rugby union coach 'a simple game for simple minds'. Because it is not generally played by those educated at public or grammar schools, it must therefore be less sophisticated and more violent. Those who broke away from the RFU must have obviously been turning away from its 'civilising process'. It is these underlying assumptions that led Eric Dunning and Ken Sheard to ride roughshod over the true historical record of northern rugby in the 1890s and present a completely false picture of the origins of rugby league. It is high time that the myth of the seventy-one deaths and all those other half-truths were swept away into the dustbin of sports history.

Notes

[1] This chapter is based on a part of a much longer article, 'History, Theory and the 'Civilising Process" *Sport in History*, v. 25, no. 2, August 2005, pp. 289-306.

[2] *Barbarians, Gentlemen and Players (BGP)* p. 187.

[3] *Pall Mall Gazette* 23 March 1892.

[4] *Pall Mall Gazette*, 30 March 1891 and 23 March 1892.

[5] *BGP*, p.248.Unfortunately, this data is incorrectly referenced in the new edition of *Barbarians, Gentleman and Players*. It is referenced as 'Sheard, 1998, p.77' but this does not match any of the works cited in the bibliography. I have therefore been unable to check the precise references.

[6] *Lancet*, 24 March 1894, p. 765.

[7] *BGP*, p. 249.

[8] *Lancet*, 24 March 1894, p. 766.

[9] *Lancet*, 16 November1907, p. 1402.

[10] For an attempt at a comprehensive list of rugby-related deaths in Yorkshire under rugby union and rugby league rules, see *Rugby's Great Spilt*, London, 1998, pp. 241 and 248.

[11] *BGP*, p. 187.

[12] *BGP*, p. 187.

[13] For Cail, see the *Yorkshire Post*, 10 February 1902. The Yorkshire Rugby Union also made the same proposal in 1898, *Yorkshire Post*, 10 October 1898.

[14] *Yorkshire Post*, 22 April 1897.

[15] *BGP*, p. 187)

[16] On the insurance difficulties of soccer, see *Athletic News*, 25 September 1911 and Matthew Taylor, *'Proud Preston' A history of the Football League 1900-39*, Unpublished PhD thesis, De Montfort University, 1997, pp. 229-30.

[17] NU General Committee minutes, 9 August 1910. The insurance scheme was set up on 29 August.

[18] Figures taken from Northern Rugby Football Union, Report and Balance Sheet, years ending 1 June 1908, 1 June 1909 and 1 June 1910.

[19] GBP, p. 245 and p. 242.

[20] On soccer, see, for example, *Athletic News*, 13 November 1917, or the memoir of Lord Kinnaird in Terence Delaney's *A Century of Soccer*, London, 1965, p. 37. On rugby, see Gus Risman, *Rugby Renegade*, (2nd edition) Leeds, 2008, p. 158. Douglas Reid, 'Folk-football the aristocracy and cultural change', *International Journal of the History of Sport*, vol. 5, no. 2, September 1988, p. 234.

7

The First Football Split:
How Soccer & Rugby Separated

Oval ball versus round ball. Two sets of goalposts. Two ways to score. Handling or kicking?

The rugby codes and soccer are so obviously and radically different today that it is difficult for modern eyes to imagine a time when they were virtually indistinguishable.

So why did the original form of football split into the soccer and rugby versions? This is a question that is asked as often as the question of why did rugby split into league and union.[1]

But in fact there was no 'original' game of football, just many variations of a game in which a ball was propelled by hand and foot towards a goal.

Whether played formally or informally, as recreation or as ritual, folk football - as the ancestors of the modern codes of football have become known - encompassed the whole of the British Isles.

It was part of the cycle of fairs, festivals and holidays in a predominantly rural British Isles. Shrove Tuesday,

Christmas Day, New Year's Day and the Easter holidays were common days for matches.

For major games football was played by large numbers, ranging from the thousand men who contested the Derby game to the 100-a-side game at Alnwick in Northumberland. Goals were three miles apart for the Ashbourne game, while Whitehaven's goals were set at the docks and a wall outside of the town. There is also some evidence of fields especially set aside for the game; for example, Hornsea, on Yorkshire's east coast, had a 'footeball grene' as far back as the 1680s.

The ball could be kicked, carried, thrown, or hit using a mixture of techniques. In Ashbourne, the ball was carried rather than kicked, and in Derby itself the game was rather descriptively called hugball. Camp-ball, the football game popular in Norfolk and Suffolk, also involved carrying of the ball. The Scone game went so far as to expressly forbid kicking the ball. In contrast, the ball was rarely picked up during the Kirkwall Ba' game in the Orkneys before the 1840s.

To those who thought that modern soccer was the sole heir to the older tradition, Montague Shearman's 1887 *Athletics and Football* commented that 'there is no trace in the original form of [football] to suggest that nothing but kicking is allowed'. Today's widespread belief that soccer is the heir to traditional folk football is not solely due to soccer's overwhelming popularity. The myth that Rugby School pupil William Webb Ellis 'created' rugby football by picking up and running with the ball - invented by the Old Rugbeian Society in 1895 - portrayed the handling code as an aberration, but it was soccer's insistence on using only feet which marked it as the deviation from the norm.

While the ways of playing football differed from area to area and time to time, there is little doubt that it was associated with the lower classes. As early as 1508

The First Football Split: How Soccer & Rugby Separated

Alexander Barclay's poem *Ecologues* wrote that 'foote-ball' was the winter pastime of the 'sturdie plowman'. The long-term survival of this link is attested to by the comment of an anonymous old Etonian, who in 1831 remarked that he could not 'consider the game of football as being at all gentlemanly. It is a game which the common people of Yorkshire are particularly partial to.' Further proof of the popularity of football can be seen in the number of recorded prosecutions for the illegal playing of informal matches down the centuries.

But the coming of urban factory-based capitalism undermined the old customs and imposed a new rhythm of daily life, destroying much of the opportunity and the inclination to play football. Although there were individual survivals of folk football, the time and work disciplines of the factory system, to say nothing of the suspicions aroused by large crowds of working people, meant that by the late 1800s, folk football was largely a historical curiosity. Some local teams did play games under their own rules, and John Gouldstone and Adrian Harvey have discovered sides dotted around the country who continued the football tradition, often with sophisticated rules.

But the impetus for the modern codes of football came from the public schools.

By the 1840s each one of the leading public schools had its own type of football. Rugby and Eton published their own rule books. The desire for public schools and their former pupils to play matches against each other led eventually to the formation of the Football Association (FA) in 1863. This was an attempt to unify the playing rules of all types of football and in this the FA failed miserably. The first draft of the FA's rules allowed handling the ball and hacking - kicking the shins - of the player in possession, but after much bureaucratic wrangling by opponents of Rugby

School football rules these were voted down and the modern game of soccer began to emerge.

In 1871 the Rugby Football Union (RFU) was formed by those clubs who supported running with the ball in the hands. Even then, the division between soccer and rugby was very indistinct and could not be compared with the codes today. Rugby until the 1880s was still primarily a kicking game and 'dribbling' the ball was a prized skill among rugby players. Association clubs initially allowed catching the ball by outfield players. Some clubs played both games and even hybrid versions of both. It was not until the two styles of football became mass spectator sports in the late 1870s that rugby and soccer could truly be said to be separate games.

The playing fields of Eton...

This view is not one that is shared by all those who have written about football's early years. In a recent book titled *Sports Histories* the sociologists Eric Dunning and Graham Curry develop an argument about the origins of the football codes that was first advanced by Dunning and Kenneth Sheard in their 1979 book about the history of rugby, *Barbarians, Gentlemen and Players*. Their belief is that the split between rugby and soccer took place much earlier and was 'set in motion principally by Eton-Rugby rivalry in the 1840s'.[2]

To support this view, *Barbarians, Gentlemen and Players* argues that

> it must have incensed the boys at Eton to have their thunder stolen by an obscure, Midlands establishment [Rugby School] which had only recently become a public school. They

considered their own to be the leading public school in *all* respects. By placing an absolute taboo on the use of hands in their version of football and decreeing that goals could only be scored under the height of the 'goal sticks', they were, one can suggest, attempting to assert their leadership of public schools and put the 'upstart' Rugbeians in their place.[3]

But this line of argument has one major defect. None of the three writers, or anyone who supports their theory, has ever been able to produce a single piece of evidence to support their idea that there was a special rivalry between Eton and Rugby schools.

Eton's major rival was Harrow school, as reflected in the annual Eton-Harrow cricket match, which by the 1840s was a major event in London's upper-class social calendar. If a similar rivalry with Rugby School existed in football, it would also have been expressed by Etonians in other spheres and activities. Yet there is no evidence for this.

The only piece of circumstantial evidence that Eric Dunning has raised is that a visit by Queen Adelaide to Rugby School in 1839 sparked Etonian rivalry towards the Midlands 'upstart'. But royal visits to Eton were regular and well-publicised events. Queen Adelaide's husband, William IV, had made one of his many visits to the school to watch a rowing contest in 1837 shortly before his death from pneumonia, causing many boys to believe his visit had caused his death. His father, George III had said of himself 'I was ever an Etonian, even from my cradle'. Queen Victoria and Prince Albert visited the school in 1841 and 1844 and donated £500 to new school buildings.

Viewed in this context, a solitary visit to Rugby school by the widow of William IV was not something that would concern even the most status-sensitive Etonian schoolboy or master.[4]

But exactly how great were the differences between the Eton and Rugby variations of football in the 1830s? Not very big at all. There is a danger of assuming that today's clear demarcation between soccer and the rugby codes is applicable to the nineteenth century. But, contrary to Dunning and Sheard's original claim that Eton placed 'an absolute taboo on the use of hands', Eton football did originally allow the use of hands to stop the ball (as Graham Curry himself has pointed out). And, although Rugby school football rules allowed carrying the ball, the game was still predominantly a kicking game, as the description of the game in *Tom Brown's Schooldays* suggests. Play was dominated by the scrum and the usual tactic was to push the scrum as far as possible before heeling the ball out to a half-back to kick for touch or, if close enough, for goal. Passing between players was very rare indeed. Matches were decided only by goals scored.

Although it would have been a matter of school pride for public schoolboys to believe that their school's form of football was unique, the reality was that the similarities were greater than the differences. The variations between Eton and Rugby rules, which are held by Dunning and Sheard to be indicators of fundamental status difference, were no greater or smaller than those of other schools. *Barbarians, Gentlemen and Players* claims that Rugby School rules' 'distinctive features such as an oval ball, 'H'-shaped goals, scoring above the cross bar, and points for tries as well as goals' were acquired between 1825 and 1850.[5]

In fact, the shape of the ball was not mentioned in the original Rugby school rules (and the RFU's rules only specified an oval ball in 1892), and the shape of the ball used in Harrow rules football, similar to a cushion, was as distinctive, if not more so, than that of Rugby. Eton's ball was much smaller than the ball subsequently used by FA clubs. And, as a glance at Victorian illustrations will show, the shape of early Rugby and Association balls was surprisingly similar to modern eyes. And although Rugby goalposts differed from Eton's, so did those of the FA - the goalposts specified in the first set of Football Association rules did not have a cross bar. Points were not awarded for tries at all until 1886, being merely the opportunity for a team to have a free kick at goal. Even the scrum, seen as a unique feature of the Rugby codes today, had its equivalents in Eton's 'bully' and Winchester's 'hot'.

Perhaps most importantly, handling the ball - seen today as a fundamental mark of the rugby codes - was common to all codes of football. Rule twenty-two of the 1847 Eton rules allowed use of the hands to stop the ball. Rule eight of the Cambridge rules of 1848 (an early attempt at a unified code of football) allowed a player to catch the ball directly from a kick and also to use his hands to stop the ball. Rule eight of the original FA rules of 1863 allowed a player to catch the ball and kick it without challenge, similar to the 'mark' in rugby or Victorian rules in Australia, as did rule three of the Sheffield Association rules of 1857, which also allowed pushing or hitting the ball with the hand. The difference between these and Rugby school rules was not handling the ball, but running with it in the hands, called 'running in' in the original Rugby School rules of 1845. But even in Rugby School rules, the ball could only be carried if it had been caught on the full and could not be picked up from the ground.[6]

What's more, if we look at how contemporary commentators viewed Eton football and its relationship to the FA's rules, and indeed the Cambridge University rules, we find no evidence to support Dunning and Sheard. The

1868 edition of C.W. Alcock's *Football Annual* carried an article 'The Chief Points of Difference of the Various Codes', detailing the many rule differences of the football codes, and did not suggest that the Eton and FA rules were similar or related. A description of the Eton game by an Old Etonian published in 1892 highlights just how different it was from soccer:

> The goals are both low and narrow, being only seven feet high and eleven feet broad, under which the ball must pass. Consequently there is no need of a regular goal-keeper, though the third behind is called 'goals'. The ball is round, made like an Association ball, but very much smaller and lighter. The proper number of players is eleven-a-side, but this number in ordinary games is often largely increased without spoiling the fun. There are eight forwards and only three behinds. ... The bully [consisting of four forwards from either side] is formed at the beginning of the game, at half-time, and, whenever the ball goes out at the side, opposite the place where it crossed the side-line and half-way to the middle of the ground; in certain cases a bully is the penalty for the infringement of a rule. ... The great principle of the game is to keep the forwards together, backing-up and on the ball. Consequently no player is allowed to touch the ball or to charge the behinds, or in any way to assist his own side or obstruct his adversaries if he is either 'sneaking' or 'cornering'. He is sneaking if he is behind the main body of his adversaries, and the ball is kicked to him or in front of him from

behind him; he is cornering when he is away from the ball, and at the side of and apart from the rest of players. The penalty for sneaking is a free kick; for cornering, a bully. Sneaking, it will be seen, roughly corresponds to off-side under Rugby Union rules, but with this exception, that the whole body of the forwards are not put out of action by the fact that the ball is kicked to them by one of their own behinds, but may charge under his kick.[7]

No wonder that Eton school boys familiar with modern soccer bemoaned the fact that their school football was *not* like that played under F.A. rules. As the novelist Henry Green remembered, looking back on his time at Eton before World War One: 'we played a medieval football in no way like any modern game except that we needed a ball and goalposts. It was a miserable substitute for soccer.'[8]

And we must also ask why, if the supporters of Eton football were the dominant force in the codification of Cambridge University and FA rules, did Etonian old boys at Cambridge form a club to play football under Eton rules in 1856? The 'Eton Club, Cambridge' continued well after the formation of the F.A., and as late as the1867-8 season played nine games against a variety of school and old boy teams.[9]

The fluidity of the various codes of football at this time can also be seen if we look at the example of Victorian (later Australian) Rules football. Its original rules predate those of the FA and RFU and appear to be a conscious mixture of Cambridge University rules and Rugby school rules. The key formulators of the game's first set of rules in 1859 in Melbourne were W.J. Hammersley and J.B. Thompson from Trinity College, Cambridge, T.H. Smith of Trinity College Dublin, where Rugby rules were played, and the old

Rugbeian Tom Wills. In some ways the rules resembled the
first FA rules in that hacking was not allowed. In others,
such as the fact that the ball could not be picked up from the
ground but could only be handled if caught on the full or on
the first bounce, they resembled Rugby rules. As Geoffrey
Blainey and Gillian Hibbins have demonstrated, however,
Australians generally thought that they were playing a
version of the game played at Rugby and in *Tom Brown's
Schooldays*, despite the fact that running with the ball was
explicitly outlawed in the 1860 version of the Melbourne
rules.[10]

... or the streets of the cities

All of these examples demonstrate that the similarities
between the various codes of football in the mid-nineteenth
century were far greater than their differences.

It is only with the benefit of hindsight that they appear to
be qualitatively different forms of football. Even the belief
that soccer and rugby could be easily divided into
'dribbling' and 'handling' codes in the middle years of the
1800s is misleading. Not only did early soccer rules allow
some use of the hands for outfield players, but dribbling the
ball was a highly-prized skill among rugby forwards until at
least World War One. One of the unfounded hopes of the
leaders of the Northern Union in the early 1900s was that the
reduction in the number of forwards from eight to six would
help to encourage more dribbling. As late as the inter-war
years it was common for the cry of 'feet Scotland, feet' to be
heard in international rugby union matches as an
encouragement to the Scots' forwards to dribble the ball.

The similarities between the early codes of football is
also illustrated by the ease with which clubs switched from
rugby to soccer in the 1870s. Preston North End and Burnley

moved from rugby to soccer in 1881 without difficulty. Many clubs played both codes in the 1870s, as well as hybrid or modified rules, despite being members of either the FA or the RFU Even the Sheffield Association played rugby-type games against Leeds and Manchester in the 1860s. William Hutchinson, the founder of the Hull football club, said that 'we played any mortal code possible with other clubs away from home so long as we could get a game of some sort'.[11] The relative indeterminacy of the rules that were played can also be seen in the example of Bramham College, a small private college in Yorkshire. The College appears to have been the first club in Yorkshire to join the FA but it had its own rules which forbade carrying the ball but allowed bouncing it (before it was introduced into Victorian rules). Nevertheless, in adult life, its pupils were instrumental in founding rugby-playing clubs in Yorkshire in the 1860s and 1870s.[12]

So why and when did the two codes diverge from each other? Fundamentally this was determined by the growing social importance of football in the 1870s, as reflected in, and stimulated by, the emergence of cup competitions. Football started to become a means by which young men could represent their city, town, village, parish, factory or street against their local rivals. And for that to happen in an organised and regular way, a common set of rules with which to play against other teams was required. This was highlighted by Sam Duckitt, the founder of the Halifax football club: 'we saw reports in the papers of football matches being played at Leeds, Bradford and elsewhere, and we thought that Halifax ought to have a club also. … We were absolutely unacquainted with the rules of either Rugby or Association. Of course, when we did commence to play, we fell in at once with the prevailing Rugby rules [in Yorkshire].'[13]

A similar phenomenon can be seen in regions where Association rules were more popular. The growth of cup, and later league, competitions was crucial in fuelling this civic rivalry and led to the divisions between the codes hardening and becoming permanent. In short, it was only when football acquired a significant role in society as a whole - and not during the essentially intra-public school debates of the early 1860s - that each code's rules hardened and the split of football into association and rugby codes could be definitively have said to have happened.

The idea that the split between soccer and rugby can be dated back to the 1840s and to the rivalry between Eton and Rugby schools is simply not supported by the facts. But, perhaps more importantly, supporters of this idea fall into the trap of using hindsight to analyse the past. By taking modern soccer and rugby as their starting point, Dunning, Sheard and Curry pick out those elements of mid-nineteenth century football that can be classified in relation to the modern versions. Thus less handling leads to soccer, more handling to rugby. Looking at history through the wrong end of the telescope causes them to emphasise the differences and downplay the many similarities of the early forms of football in order to fit their preconceptions about modern soccer and rugby.

Despite rightly attacking the William Webb Ellis story of rugby's origins as a myth, their aim is ultimately to discover the 'true source' of modern soccer, unintendedly echoing of Matthew Bloxam's quest to find the boy who 'invented' Rugby football. Just as Bloxam drew a line from Webb Ellis to rugby in his day, Dunning and Curry's work seeks to draw a straight line from the Eton football rules of 1847 to today's multi-billion pound soccer industry. And in doing so, they fall into exactly the same trap as Bloxam by making claims about the past for which no evidence can be found.

The First Football Split: How Soccer & Rugby Separated

It took many years for the true facts of the 1895 rugby split to re-emerge. It would be a tragedy if the origins of football's first split between soccer and rugby were to be similarly lost in the mists of time and myth-making.

Notes

[1] This chapter is based on a part of a much longer article, 'History, Theory and the 'Civilising Process'' *Sport in History*, v. 25, n. 2, August 2005, pp. 289-306.

[2] Eric Dunning and Graham Curry, 'Public Schools, Status Rivalry and the development of football' in Eric Dunning, Dominic Malcolm and Ivan Waddington (eds), *Sport Histories. Figurational Studies of the Development of Modern Sports*, London: Routledge, 2004, p. 47.

[3] Eric Dunning and Kenneth Sheard, *Barbarians, Gentlemen and Players: A Sociological Study of the Development of Rugby Football*, Second Edition, London: Routledge, 2005, p. 86.

[4] Eric Dunning, 'The origins of modern football and the public school ethos', in B. Simon and I. Bradley (eds) *The Victorian Public School*, Dublin, 1975, p. 175. Tim Card, *Eton Established. A history from 1440 to 1860*, London, 2001, pp. 156, 108, 155 and 149.

[5] *Barbarians, Gentlemen and Players*, p. 52.

[6] For Eton see Dunning and Curry, p. 44.

[7] S.R. James 'Eton Football' in Rev. Frank Marshall (ed.), *Football, The Rugby Union Game*, 2nd Edition, London, 1894, pp. 32-3.

[8] Henry Green, *Pack My Bag* (London, 1940; new edition published in 1952). p. 92.

[9] See C.W. Alcock (ed.) *Football Annual*, London, 1868, pp. 19 and 42.

[10] For Australian Rules, see Geoffrey Blainey, *A Game Of Our Own: the origins of Australian football*, 2nd Edition, Melbourne, 2003, pp. 222-4, and G. M. Hibbins, 'The Cambridge Connection: The English Origins of Australian Rules Football' in J. A. Mangan (ed.) *The Cultural Bond. Sport, Empire, Society*. London, 1993.

[11] *Yorkshire Evening Post*, 1 December 1900.

[12] For Bramham College rules, see the *Bramham College Magazine*, November 1864, p. 182. The school is listed as a member of the FA in the *Football Annual* of 1870.

[13] *Yorkshire Evening Post*, 9 February 1901.

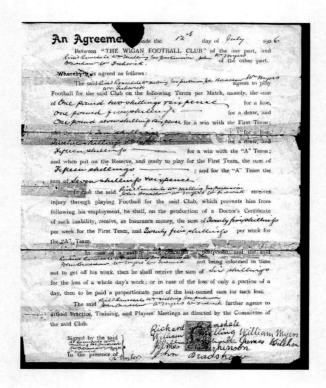

The earliest existing rugby league contract from 1906

8

Rugby's Great Purge:
What Happened To Rugby Union After 1895?

The idea that a sport could turn its back on thousands of players, rid itself of hundreds of clubs and hunt down those who it saw as its enemies is unthinkable to us in the twenty-first century.[1] Today, every sport wants more players, more clubs and more spectators.

But a hundred years ago, in the years after rugby's great split in 1895, the attitude of the Rugby Football Union was very different. Then, the RFU did not seek popularity, increased participation levels nor the expansion of rugby. Its goal was simple: to defend and extend the amateur basis of rugby union.

The evolution of the RFU following the 1895 split followed the classic pattern of all civil wars. Ruthless victory over the opposition was followed by purging all remaining supporters of the insurrection, those seen as compromisers and not a few 'innocent' victims. Once the potential for future rebellions had finally been extinguished, the victors the turned their attention to their project of reconstruction, untrammelled by the restrictions of the past. And to achieve its goals, the RFU was prepared to reduce the game to a level that had not been seen for over a generation.

The 'Fit But Few' Principle

Although the leaders of rugby union claimed that amateurism was an ancient tradition as old as the game itself, in fact amateurism in rugby was a mere nine years old when the split with the northern clubs took place in 1895.[2]

The first amateur regulations had only been introduced by the RFU in 1886, fifteen years after its foundation, and were an explicit attempt to curb the influence of working-class players within the game. As well as being worried by the huge influx of working-class players and spectators into the game in the north of England, the leaders of the RFU had been chastened by the experience of the Football Association, whose legalisation of professionalism in the early 1880s had led to the rapid eclipse of the amateur teams of former public schoolboys that had hitherto dominated the FA Cup.

'Professionalism' quickly became a code word for concern about the growing influence of working-class players in rugby. The RFU's 1886 regulations forbade payments in cash or in kind to players and punished violators with suspension or expulsion from the game. For the major clubs in Lancashire and Yorkshire, whose crowds and commercial interests matched and sometimes surpassed those of leading soccer clubs, the threat of the loss of players or fixtures due to the zealous pursuit of what was known as 'veiled professionalism' endangered their success and economic viability.

Even so, the RFU continued to tighten its amateur regulations. The northern clubs' call for the legalisation of 'broken time' payments, compensation to players who had to take time off work to play, was voted down at the 1893 annual general meeting of the RFU. In 1895 the RFU leadership announced plans to introduce a rule that would mean any club accused of professionalism would have to prove its innocence to avoid suspension. Faced with this declaration of war, in August 1895 twenty-two of the north's leading clubs broke away and formed the Northern Union. Over the next six years the vast majority of rugby clubs in Yorkshire, Lancashire and Cumberland joined them.

The driving out of the northern clubs gave the RFU leadership what it had wanted. As Frank Mitchell, dual cricket and rugby international, explained:

> ...the working-man player has not taught us anything in the way of style or skill in playing the game. Physique and stamina above the average he undoubtedly has, but to say that he knows more about the game than one who has been brought up in the best traditions of the public schools and the universities is absurd. If in any way the game has improved his physical and mental capacity, we are more than repaid; but at the same time, if he cannot play the game for the game itself, he can have no true interest in it, and it were better that he left us.[3]

At its September 1895 annual general meeting, held four weeks after the split, the RFU had sought to draw a clear line between itself and the NU. It rigorously defined what constituted professionalism:

> asking, receiving, or replying to a promise, direct or implied, to receive any money consideration

whatever, actual or prospective; any employment
or advancement; any establishment in business; or
any compensation whatever [for playing, training
or 'rendering any service' to a club][4]

The new professionalism rules carried on through twenty-
seven clauses and a further twelve sub-clauses. As well as
forbidding the acceptance or provision of any form of
payment or inducement to play the game, the rules
categorised as 'acts of professionalism' testimonial funds,
playing in a benefit match of any type, officiating in a match
taking place on the ground of an expelled club, and refusing
to give evidence to the RFU committee. The provisions
relating to clubs were just as stringent. As well as this mesh
of regulation, the RFU also adopted a codicil that declared
all members of NU clubs, whether paid or not, to be
professionals, and barred rugby union teams and players
from playing on NU grounds. Those unfortunates who were
members of NU clubs but wished to retain their amateur
status were given until 1 November 1895 to resign from their
clubs.

Despite the RFU's desire for an airtight seal against the
professional virus, the new regulations carried inherent
problems. Although it forbade compensation for 'time lost
to football or in traveling in connection with football', in the
very next clause it explicitly allowed the payment of
'reasonable hotel or traveling expenses', offering the
potential of practical ambiguity to those seeking a way
around the regulations. More importantly, the rules seemed
to violate logic by condemning as professionals even those
members of NU clubs who did not receive monetary or
other recompense for playing the game. Like original sin,
professionalism was now a stain which could mark those
whose lives had been exemplary - indeed, the rugby union

player who received traveling expenses was deemed to be more 'amateur' than the NU player who received no expenses.

But that should not have been surprising. Despite the centrality of the concept to the sport, the RFU's rules never defined amateurism nor what constituted an amateur. The term was defined only in the negative, as being the opposite of professionalism, which was categorised to an obsessive degree by the RFU rule makers. It was very clear what amateurism was *not*, but what it *was* proved to be somewhat more slippery. The rugby journalist Philip Trevor linked it to the 'public school spirit' but acknowledged the essential flexibility of the term: 'of course, we cannot define the term 'public school spirit' any more than we can define, by any amount of elaboration, the term 'gentleman'. But we all know exactly what we mean by both.'[5] Thus, for rugby union, amateurism was not a fixed concept but one that shifted its meaning according to the circumstances in which the RFU found itself at any given time.

So the main concern of the rugby union authorities, both nationally and locally, became not so much on whether a player had received money to play rugby but the extent of his contact with the NU. After the split it was hoped by RFU loyalists in the north that players who had played as amateurs with NU clubs might be eligible to play for rugby union clubs, provided they had severed their connections with the NU. This quickly proved to be a vain hope and the RFU insisted that playing rugby for an NU club was itself an act of professionalism, regardless of whether money had changed hands, and that the sinner be cast out.

As a concession, the RFU initially allowed players who signed for an NU club, but did not play or receive any money, to be reinstated. This was a very small group indeed, yet in March 1901 the RFU changed its mind and decided that even this group did not deserve its sympathy. Henceforth players who merely signed a Northern Union registration form were banned for life from playing rugby union. This draconian stance served to underline the fact that the RFU no longer defined amateurism in relation to payments for play; it was simply whatever the NU was not. The NU was now officially and unshakably the 'Other'.

The policy caused considerable heartache among the RFU's loyal supporters among the northern middle classes. From East Yorkshire A.R. Meek protested that the RFU's banishment of 'genuine amateurs' who had played amateur NU because there were no local RFU clubs 'is fast bringing the historic pastime into ridicule'. The Sugden brothers, scions of one of Brighouse's leading families and 'amateurs in the strictest sense of the word', resigned from Brighouse Rangers in protest against the NU's legalisation of full professionalism in 1898. Yet they too were refused permission to play rugby union because they had 'professionalised' themselves. In Lancashire the Vale of Lune club committee protested to the RFU in 1902 about the refusal to allow two players who 'are landed proprietors, and may figure in Burke's [Peerage]' to play the union game because they had previously played in a local amateur NU side because it was the only rugby club in their locality. But the RFU insisted on the letter of its law being obeyed.[6]

Despite the seeming illogicality of purging players who shared the sporting ideals and social status of its leaders, there was method in its madness. The RFU leadership was determined to carry out a scorched earth policy to prevent the possibility of professionalism arising anew in the north. In order to remove once and for all the threat of working-class dominance, compromise could not be countenanced. Moreover, many in the central leadership of the RFU blamed the rise of professionalism in the north on the inability or unwillingness of the middle classes to provide firm leadership to working-class players. So, for example, at the 1895 general meeting, RFU secretary Rowland Hill hoped forlornly that 'those who have real social influence amongst the working classes of this country will use it to point out the evils which I am convinced are before them' and the Reverend Frank Marshall denounced 'men of superior intelligence' who 'pandered to the claims of their clubs and their working-men players'.[7]

The impact of the RFU's policy – described by the cricket and rugby journalist A.W. Pullin as 'the fit but few principle' - can be seen with stunning clarity in its membership figures.[8] On the eve of the 1895 split the RFU had 416 adult clubs in membership, excluding schools, colleges and universities. Of these, 147 were in Yorkshire and 51 in Lancashire, almost 48 per cent of the total. But ten years later the number of adult clubs in England that belonged to the RFU had plummeted to just 155, of which a mere five were in Yorkshire and fourteen in Lancashire. By 1910 the total had inched up to 176, with the former powerhouse of Yorkshire adding just one more club to its total.[9]

'Evil Times'

The devastating effect of the RFU's policies could also be seen on the pitch. Between 1890 and 1895 England won eleven of eighteen matches against Ireland, Scotland and Wales. With the exception of the 1895 matches, when pre-split manoeuvrings led the RFU to select only two players from future NU clubs, there were never less than four players in the England side from clubs that would break away in 1895. Indeed, the 1892 team, which did the 'Grand Slam' to win the international championship for the first time since 1884, never had less than eight such players in the side, with the team that defeated Scotland in the final match of the championship having ten. In all, almost forty-three per cent of the players who played for England between 1890 and 1894 came from clubs or would join clubs that went on to form the NU.

But in the five seasons following the split, England won just four, and drew two, out of fifteen matches, as clubs in the north abandoned the RFU for the NU. Writing in 1898 Philip Trevor noted that 'amateur rugby football has fallen upon evil times'.[10] Even worse was to come. Between 1901 and 1909 England won just six, and drew one, of twenty-seven matches with the three home nations. The continual defeats suffered by England in the 1900s became a testimony to the RFU's sacrifice and steel in upholding the amateur banner. The comment of New Zealand's Dave Gallaher and Billy Stead, that 'it is better that a game should be played badly, and that none should go to see it, than that the price should have to be paid for professionalism' encapsulated the attitude of the RFU, if not necessarily their own.[11]

These self-inflicted wounds were exacerbated by financial difficulties and the impact of soccer on the game. Although the RFU believed that its amateurism made it immune from the pressure of commercial forces, this was not the case. In 1895 the patrician Manchester club had voted to disband due to financial difficulties, although the decision was later rescinded. In 1898 the Broughton club, also in Manchester and one of the oldest in Lancashire, disbanded because in the words of its president, it was 'not in a position to pay its way'.[12]

In 1897 the Durham union sought to form a league to stimulate public interest in the face of soccer's runaway popularity in the region. When the RFU committee discussed the proposal the following year, they unsurprisingly refused to sanction the idea, and also refused to support a similar league that had been formed in Cornwall. Durham's neighbours in the Northumberland union also opposed the idea, believing that it would 'mean the extinction of rugby north of the Tyne', despite the fact that, with only five clubs in membership, the Northumberland union was not too far from extinction itself.[13]

It was perhaps a belated sense of self-awareness, heightened by South Shields' defection to the NU in 1901, that led the Northumbrians in 1902 to propose the introduction of a national rugby cup competition. As Pullin noted 'the popularity of the Association game in and around Newcastle and Sunderland, and the encroachment of the Northern Union, with its threatened developments, appear to have raised in certain Rugby unionists the necessity of attempting something in the direction of popularising their own game in the North East'.[14]

The RFU's studied indifference to the fate of the game in the North East led to a steady stream of clubs disbanding. In 1904 Tudhoe, one of the few remaining clubs with a working-class following in Durham, folded after a 'financially disastrous' season, followed in 1906 by Blaydon Wanderers, one of the county's oldest clubs. In response to this decline, Northumberland's Rockcliff club proposed to the 1904 RFU AGM that the scoring system should be changed to make the scoring of tries more important than goals, similar to the NU system, in order to increase the game's appeal, but it fell by the wayside due to a lack of interest among other clubs.[15]

The following year Sunderland RFC, one of the oldest clubs in the region, discussed switching to soccer because 'the gates at the rugby matches have been of the most meagre character and, outside the members of the club, very few people seem to have been taking any interest in the fixtures', despite arranging their matches so as not clash with those of Sunderland AFC.[16] This steady contraction of the game in the North East culminated in 1908 when West Hartlepool, which despite being arguably the region's best side had been losing money since at least 1902, disbanded and reformed itself as Hartlepools United AFC.[17] Writing in the same year, the collapse of the union game in the North was captured by a returning member of the 1905 New Zealand All Black side:

> In the northern counties I find nearly a total abolition [of rugby union]. All round it seems retrogression. The causes are too various to mention. The masses have never been catered for and the game is not to their liking. They have been ignored and prejudiced and their support dwindled. Only the upper classes, colleges, universities etc have been studied and the game remains with them.[18]

This retrogression was not just confined to the North. In all of the remaining areas in which rugby union retained a modicum of a working-class support it struggled to retain its popularity in the face of the soccer behemoth. At the RFU's 1900 annual general meeting Bristol District RFU asked permission to form a local league to counter the growth of soccer in the city. Rugby 'was being killed by the competition of the association game' declared one of the Bristol delegates, adding that 'if the resolution was not carried, the younger portion of players would go over to the association code'.

Despite this heartfelt plea, the resolution was lost, although the desperate Bristolians went ahead and formed a league, the Bristol Combination, anyway. In Devon the need to counteract the sudden popularity of soccer led to the formation of a league structure in defiance of the RFU.[19]

Such was the enthusiasm for the round-ball code that it had even begun to threaten rugby union in its more middle-class strongholds. In 1904 Frank Potter-Irwin of the Ilford Wanderers club, a future vice-president of the RFU, described how 'the Rugby Union included something like 250 clubs, whereas in his own district there were 247 association clubs'. He appealed to the RFU 'to give up its antiquated methods and do something to popularise the game.'[20]

Of course, 'popularising' rugby was the very opposite of what the central leadership of the RFU wanted to do. But the rapid decline of the sport's fortunes in England both on and off the pitch presented the RFU leadership with a dilemma. Its ferocity in pursuing the evil of professionalism was threatening to undermine its public credibility as a major national sport, yet no matter how hard it tried, it could not finally cast out the incubus.

As the 1900s progressed, the RFU became increasingly divided between purifiers, who would stop at nothing in their pursuit of spotless amateurism, and pragmatists, whose amateur ideals were tempered by the need to maintain the organisational strength of the RFU. To some extent this reflected a difference over how to deal with the working class in rugby. The purists wanted complete separation from the working class, whereas the pragmatists were quite prepared to allow working-class participation provided that working-class players knew their place in the social hierarchy and did not present a threat to the leadership of the RFU and its principles. Nowhere was this tension more apparent than in the ongoing controversies over allegations of professionalism among Midlands clubs.

'A question of expediency'

After the socially prestigious clubs of London and the working-class rugby strongholds of Lancashire and Yorkshire, Leicester was the biggest club in English rugby. But since the mid-1890s it had been constantly suspected of paying players and offering them inducements to join it. The club itself, with its well-appointed ground, large crowds and rigorous team selection policies, which paid no heed to the 'clubability' displayed by southern sides, seemed to resemble an NU club more than it did its allies in the RFU. In February 1896 the team had been subject to an RFU inquiry about its signing of A.C. Butlin from Rugby RFC. Although it was found not guilty, former RFU president William Cail told the press that 'Leicester had had a bad name for poaching and using undue influence but they had come out of the inquiry clean'.[21]

Nevertheless, suspicions remained, not least among NU clubs who suspected that the RFU turned a blind eye to Leicester's indiscretions in order not to force them into the arms of the NU. The rugby culture of the city was also viewed with raised eyebrows by RFU purists. By 1904 the local league had five divisions and the offering of jobs and other inducements to players by clubs was a widespread, if covert, practice.[22]

In January 1907, in an attempt to put an end to the professional miasma that hung over Leicester and other leading Midlands sides such as Coventry, the RFU formed a 'Commission on Veiled Professionalism', and invited any interested party to submit evidence to it. The commission took over a year to report, visiting Bristol, Hartlepool Hull, Leicester, Manchester, Plymouth and York to take evidence, during which time Coventry, Leicester and Northampton had been openly accused of paying players by Moseley club secretary James Byrne.

When the report was published, it presented a litany of abuses of the RFU's amateur regulations, including unaudited accounts, vague balance sheets, expenses being paid without receipts, 'unnecessary refreshments' for players and one case of a player actually being offered money to remain at a club. Despite this, the report concluded by incongruously stating that 'so far as they could ascertain ... veiled professionalism did not now exist in the Rugby Union game'![23]

The somewhat startling disjuncture between the findings of the report and its conclusion enraged the supporters of absolute purification. Byrne and fellow members of his Birmingham Old Edwardians club, submitted a motion to that year's RFU AGM declaring themselves 'not satisfied that 'veiled professionalism' does not exist in the Rugby Union,' and viewing 'with alarm the attitude of the Rugby Union towards the whole question'. At the meeting itself Byrne tore into the RFU, pointedly asking that if there was no veiled professionalism why were Leicester and Northampton told to ask players to refund payments that had apparently been made to them. Supporting Byrne, Sam Tattersall of Yorkshire asked why Leicester had not been suspended for fielding a former NU player, an offence which had led to the expulsion of clubs in Yorkshire. Byrne's motion was lost by just nine votes.[24]

Stung by its narrow escape, the RFU committee sought to appease the purifiers and appointed a sub-committee to look into the work of the Commission on Veiled Professionalism. Almost buckling under pressure, it then announced another inquiry into accusations of professionalism against Leicester, while at the same time voting down a counterposed motion calling for Leicester to be expelled. Four players were suspended for allegedly having played NU football. But, when the inquiry reported back in January 1909, it amazingly cleared Leicester of all charges of veiled professionalism.

This was too much for the purifiers. RFU president Charles Crane promptly resigned his post, complaining that the RFU's stance was 'rather an encouragement of professionalism rather than an effort to eradicate it'. Byrne responded by sending a circular to clubs claiming that the RFU was refusing to act against any case of professionalism unless the evidence was overwhelming and calling on it to implement the letter of its own laws. At that year's RFU AGM, a motion from Byrne calling on the RFU to expel the guilty Midlands clubs was overwhelmingly defeated by 189 to 11 votes on the recommendation of Rowland Hill who urged pragmatism and a policy of expediency. To pass such a motion, he advised, 'would be to practically break up the union'.[25]

Once again, the RFU leadership's ambiguity towards amateurism allowed it to shift its position according to its broader needs. And in the case of Leicester it was prepared to ignore the evidence because the situation in the East Midlands did not threaten its authority. Indeed, the opposite was the case. As Hill warned, to have imposed a literal reading of its regulations would have meant the expulsion of Leicester and the prospect of the NU establishing a serious bridgehead in the Midlands.

This pragmatism was well-illustrated by the events surrounding the Coventry club. Perhaps even more so than Leicester, rugby union in Coventry had a significant working-class following.[26] But the club lacked the size and the social cachet of its East Midlands rival, and, possibly as a concession to the 'purifying' element in the sport, in late September 1909 the RFU began an investigation into claims that the club had covertly made payments to its players.

On 6 October Coventry was found guilty of

professionalism and suspended until the beginning of 1910. The club secretary was permanently expelled from rugby union for his part in organising the payments and five players were suspended. Even the club's ground could not be used until the new year. The following week rumours emerged that club officials had met with the NU with a view to switching codes. For the next few weeks the club debated its future, with a significant faction wanting to join the NU as soon as possible and another waiting to see if the RFU executive would reduce the length of the club's suspension before deciding on their future course of action.

Tired of waiting for a decision from the RFU, the pro-NU faction called a meeting for 29 November to establish the Coventry NU club. Faced with the prospect of the NU club capturing public attention while the union side was still suspended, the RFU suddenly declared on 6 December that the sanctions against the union club had been lifted and that it was free to start playing again, thus once again demonstrating the flexibility of its principles.[27]

As the episodes in the Midlands demonstrated, the RFU leadership was perfectly prepared to turn a blind eye to violations of its amateur code when it did not feel that such actions would threaten its position or goals. This was especially true at an international level. The RFU saw itself as playing a crucial role in English national sporting life through the organisation of the annual Four Nations championship, and from 1905 through regular visits from teams from the white Dominions of the British Empire, Australia, New Zealand and South Africa.

The public and media attention given to these contests not only gave the RFU a national prominence but also seemed to demonstrate the vitality of middle-class sport during a period in which professional soccer seemed to be constantly reaching new peaks of popularity. The avoidance of any diminution of its national influence and the preservation of what it came to see as its imperial role led the RFU to take a more accommodating position towards what in other circumstances it would have unhesitatingly have condemned as professionalism.

Most famously this was the case in Wales. In 1896 Arthur Gould, the greatest Welsh player of his generation, had been the recipient of a hugely successful testimonial organised by the Welsh rugby union authorities, the proceeds of which were used to purchase, and present him with, the deeds to his house in Newport. Initially the RFU declared this to be an act of professionalism. In February 1897, the International Board endorsed the RFU position and, in protest, the Welsh withdrew from the Board. A split appeared to be imminent.

However, in September 1897, the RFU flip-flopped and declared that, although Gould was guilty of professionalism, 'the exceptional circumstances' of his case meant that he would not be expelled from the game. Rowland Hill admitted openly that the decision 'was a question of expediency', arguing that it would be 'a serious strain on the loyalty of the West Country clubs of England if those fixtures [against Welsh sides] were prohibited'. F.E. Smith candidly admitted in *The Times* that a compromise had been reached to 'prevent the great accession of strength to the Northern Union which would have followed had the Welsh Union been driven into their arms'.[28]

The preservation of the link with Wales was paramount to the RFU. Coming barely two years after the split with the northern clubs, a definitive break with the Welsh, which would have inevitably resulted in the Northern and Welsh unions joining together in a semi-professional British rugby union, would have been a body blow to the RFU's prestige and national authority from which it would have been difficult to recover. As a fig-leaf, the RFU barred Gould from playing or refereeing outside of Wales, a measure the rugby correspondent of *Country Life* characterised as 'absurd', given that he could play or referee in matches involving English sides in Wales but not those involving Welsh sides in England.[29]

Similarly absurd contortions took place a decade later when in 1908, the RFU found its amateur fealty being questioned by the leaders of Scottish rugby union. The Scots had traditionally seen themselves as the upholders of the true spirit of rugby, both in the playing of the game and in devotion to amateurism. They had been deeply troubled by the 1905 All Blacks tour and argued strenuously that regular payments of expenses to touring players (which in the All Blacks' case was three shillings per day) was a form of wage and therefore professionalism.[30] In 1907 they had asked to see the accounts of the 1905 tour, which seem not to have been forthcoming, and in March 1908 they had even suspended one of their own players, Tom Wilson, for accepting a place on the 1908 Anglo-Welsh tour of New Zealand on the grounds that he would be paid regular expenses.

As with the English purifiers, Scottish discontent had smouldered for some time and it was the one guinea (twenty-one shillings) a week payment to Australian players on their 1908-09 UK tour that brought things to a head. Unable to persuade the RFU to act, the Scots abruptly announced on 12 January 1909 that they would not play their scheduled match against England in March. When it came to amateurism, 'there can be no halfway house in Rugby football,' Scottish secretary James Smith sternly instructed the RFU.[31]

As many commentators pointed out, the three shillings per day payment was the same as had been paid on the 1904 British rugby union tour of Australasia, which had been captained by a Scotsman, David Bedell-Sivright. Some even highlighted the fact that a guinea a week was considerably more than the six shillings per week broken-time allowance that the Northern Union had sanctioned in 1895. RFU secretary C.J.B. Marriott claimed in a letter to the Scots that the three shillings a day was merely an allowance to cover drinks taken with meals, perhaps giving an insight into the sobriety of touring teams, but less than a fortnight later the RFU back-tracked slightly and decided that, although three shillings per day was not an unreasonable amount, in the future it should not be paid directly to players.

This concession seems to have placated the Scots somewhat and in February the International Board resolution declared that 'the making of any allowance to players in cash is contrary to the principles of amateur Rugby football, and in future no such allowance be made to any player'.[32] The dispute thus ended in time for the England-Scotland match to take place and the Calcutta Cup to be carried home by a victorious Scots team.[33]

'The more public school men get to play our game, the better we are'

As the dispute with the Scots demonstrated, the impact of the All Blacks on British rugby and the RFU in particular, followed by subsequent tours by South Africa and Australia, was inherently contradictory. The success of the New Zealanders and the spectacle of what appeared to be the Empire's finest athletes playing rugby union added to the RFU's prestige and significantly increased the national profile of the sport, allowing it to claim to be the winter sport of the Empire, and vindicating its defence of the amateur code and its opposition to professionalism.

But, as Greg Ryan has documented, beneath the surface

many supporters of the RFU were not comfortable with the way that the New Zealanders played the game nor with the discrepancy between the rhetoric and the reality of their amateurism. It was felt by many that their play was too organised, too planned and too systematic; in short, it bordered on professionalism. And, as the Scots later pointed out, the payment of three shillings a day expenses resembled nothing so much as 'broken time' payments. It was no surprise that the RFU dismissed out of hand in February 1906 a call from Australia for the formation of an Imperial governing body for rugby.[34]

The Anglo-Welsh tour to Australia and New Zealand of 1908 - organised in part to counter the spread of rugby league in the Southern Hemisphere - only served to emphasise the gap between the rugby cultures of the imperial centre and its periphery. It was boycotted by the Scots and Irish, and when the side arrived in New Zealand the RFU hastily banned one of the tourists, Frederick Jackson, because it had discovered that he had played rugby league for Swinton. Dogged by accusations and counter-accusations of gamesmanship and rough play, the tour failed miserably to stop the advance of the rival game.[35]

But if the RFU was uncomfortable with developments abroad, at home it was free to pursue a policy that was designed to remove any aspect of uneasiness about the culture or social composition of the game. The weeding out of the clubs in the north that drew their support and playing strength from the working class allowed the RFU to rebuild the game in its own image by 'encourag[ing] the class of players who hitherto have been elbowed out in the evolution of professionalism'.[36] In the north, new clubs were established that proudly announced their social origins. Old Dewsburians were founded by 'the sons of better-class Dewsbury and Batley residents'; Hull and East Riding was set up by 'the sons of Hull and district's leading citizens'; and the Leigh club was the creation of 'past and present university men residing in the neighbourhood'.[37]

The decline in the number of clubs in the RFU also had the effect of strengthening the power of those sides based on the middle classes. Although the number of clubs based on old boys' teams, the professions or the schools did not rise significantly, those that existed were now proportionally far stronger. And clubs in the Midlands and the South West that still had working-class support certainly did not challenge, explicitly or implicitly, the hierarchy of the RFU. Indeed, because they now posed no threat, the presence of working-class players was something to be cautiously welcomed, signifying a re-establishment of an idealised social pyramid of patronage and deference.

By the mid-1900s, confident that it had vanquished its opponents and secure in its position as the most prominent promoter of amateurism in British sport, the RFU began to look at increasing the popularity of the sport. In 1904, in response to a campaign by the NU to establish the game in schools, James Mawson of the Furness club in Barrow had written to the RFU encouraging them to set up schoolboy competitions. In the north, the Yorkshire Rugby Union established an invitational side, the Yorkshire Wanderers, to promote the game in local public and grammar schools. In the Midlands an English Schools Rugby Union was founded to promote the game in state schools.

In 1906 the RFU wrote to all the major non-rugby playing public schools asking them to give rugby a try, warning darkly of 'the danger of young men been driven to look on at games between paid-for men,' a not so subtle attack on soccer, and going on to stress that 'the game of Rugby football has always been at its best when good players were available from our Public Schools, and the more Public School men get to play our game, the better we are certain it is for it'.[38]

The RFU also turned its attention to the army. Despite its strident advocacy of the moral benefits of amateurism and its role in maintaining good imperial relations with the Dominions, rugby union was a very distant second to soccer as the winter sport of the armed forces. Indeed, in 1906 the RFU had been contacted by rugby-playing officers in the army with a plea to assist them in organising rugby matches. It was felt that part of the problem was that many potential players among servicemen were forbidden to play because they had links with Northern Union clubs. Rowland Hill therefore proposed lifting the ban on NU players who were serving in the military. As he had done over the Gould affair and the Leicester compromise, he claimed his proposal had to be supported 'in the interests of the game'. Despite opposition, his motion was carried and the RFU offered trophies to the army and navy if they organised rugby tournaments. As if to confirm the efficacy of the RFU's lifting of the ban on NU players, the inaugural army cup contest was won by a regiment from the West Riding of Yorkshire, the seat of the rebellion in 1895.[39]

Although promoting the game in the schools and the armed forces did not bring great numbers into the sport - but it did sow the seeds of the eventual 'rush to rugby' in the 1920s - it helped to infuse the sport with a renewed sense of self-confidence. This was reflected in the change in the fortunes of the national side. From 1910 the transformation of the England team could not have been more marked. After a generation of failure, in the five years from 1910 England won sixteen matches and lost just three, finishing top of the Five Nations table four times and completed successive 'Grand Slams' in 1913 and 1914.

This success was based firmly on players from the public

schools and the exclusive London clubs and founded on the attacking three-quarter play that had been introduced by England and Harlequins' captain Adrian Stoop, who had been inspired by the combination play of the 1905 All Blacks. Following Stoop's retirement from the international side in 1912 the system continued with even greater success, embodied in his successor as captain, Ronald Poulton-Palmer.[40] As England resurrected the image of the dashing public school three-quarter who could score tries at will, the mythic appeal of the game to the middle classes was re-established. The fact that both Stoop and Poulton-Palmer were former pupils of Rugby School seemed to offer historical justification for the correctness of the path that the RFU had followed since 1895.

Pure and Simple Amateurism?

The concerns of the RFU following the split mirror those of broader middle-class society of the period. The first decade of the twentieth century was a period of increasing self-doubt among the upper and middle classes in Britain. The imperial certainties of Victorian times had been brought into question by the difficulties of the Boer War, economic self-confidence had been sapped by the eclipse of British industrial power by the United States and Germany, and domestically the traditional social hierarchy of British society had begun to be undermined by the rise of the labour movement. In this environment of uncertainty, social values and mores often became a shield with which to keep the forces of change at bay.

As Samuel Hynes noted, the Edwardian age was an age of propriety, when conventional middle-class standards of behaviour became 'rigid and empty gestures of decorum, important not because they implied moral rightness, but because they seemed to protect social stability, public morals, religion, and the British Empire against the threat of change'.[41] Within this decaying fabric of decorum, amateurism was a vital and highly visible thread in maintaining the signs and symbols of control. Most importantly, it allowed the sport to claim a moral authority over professional sports, especially soccer and rugby league.

But in reality, the policies and actions of the RFU offered no support for the belief that amateurism was morally superior to sports that allowed payments to players. For those for whom amateurism was meant to protect and reassure, the RFU's regulations presented sufficient opportunities for practices that its critics claimed were hypocritical. The allowing of travel expenses offered considerable leeway for abuse, something that had been a constant complaint of northern clubs before the 1895 split. Even a confirmed supporter of the RFU and its policies such as E.H.D. Sewell was forced to admit that the payment of travel expenses was a well known means of providing 'men of higher social standing [with] a free Easter or Christmas holiday'.[42]

The offering of inducements to switch clubs, often cited by supporters of the RFU as a primary evil in the north before the split and a focus for investigations in the 1900s, was also no less an issue among the socially-elite clubs in London than it was for those lower down the social ladder. As early as 1890, complaints had surfaced about the recruitment activities of Blackheath, who had managed to recruit an array of talented players from their rivals in London. The issue had arisen again at the annual general meeting of the Middlesex RFU in 1898, when some of the smaller clubs had expressed concerns at the regularity with which their most talented players left to play for the leading London clubs.[43] Of course, the difference was that money rarely, if ever, changed hands because a move to a more prestigious London club brought with it intangible social, employment and business benefits to the fortunate player.

Moreover, and more damaging to the RFU's claim to moral leadership, the web of amateur regulation was so dense and contradictory that many players simply resorted to lying to avoid becoming entangled. A.W. Robinson, a former Keighley and Hull KR player who had moved to Stourbridge to take up a job as a teacher, played under a pseudonym for his local rugby union club until an zealous RFU supporter unmasked him. When confronted with evidence that they had played for Hull Marlborough NU club, some members of the Hull and East Riding rugby union side simply denied any knowledge of NU rugby at all. Manchester Free Wanderers were suspended for fielding an NU player by the Lancashire county rugby union despite being told to 'play him and say nothing' by a prominent member of the county committee.[44]

And there were also the generous expenses paid to RFU officials. Members of the Yorkshire Rugby Union committee travelled to meetings by first-class rail, a privilege refused to those who merely played the game. A testimonial match for Lancashire and RFU president Roger Westray was organised to reward his long service to the game, something that was explicitly forbidden to players by the RFU.[45] It is therefore unsurprising that the RFU was regularly accused of dishonesty and double standards by its opponents. The RFU, claimed a critic in 1909,

> turn out bag and baggage all players who wish to be recompensed for loss of working time and consequent loss of wages, and the next they are willing to 'allow' sums of 12s or 21s a week for what are euphoniously described as 'personal

and petty expenses'... what is professionalism in a working man is evidently something very different in a player of slightly superior social status.[46]

This was precisely the point. Although there were differences and even disputes over the definition and implementation of amateurism within rugby union, all parties shared the position that that working-class participation had to be subordinated to the control of the middle classes. The removal of the perceived danger that the sport could become dominated by the working classes on or off the field - and the consequent destruction of a gentlemanly social environment which such a development would entail - was the primary motivating force in all of the debates on amateurism within the RFU.

One indicator of the success of the RFU in changing the balance of forces within rugby in favour of the middle classes can be seen in the shift in the class composition of the England national team. Between 1890 and 1894, 36.1 per cent of England players whose occupations can be traced came from a manual labouring background. But in the last five years of the Edwardian period, 1906-1910, that percentage had fallen to 13.8 per cent.[47] By 1914, what working-class participation that remained in English rugby union was deferential, non-threatening and strictly controlled. The game was now unquestionably dominated by gentlemen.

In the penultimate chapter of Anthony Trollope's *The Last Chronicle of Barset* Josiah Crawley laments to Archdeacon Grantly, who is about to become his daughter's father-in-law, that he is not his financial equal. But Grantly reassures him. 'We stand,' he replied, 'on the perfect level on which men can meet each other. We are both gentlemen.' It was that quest for the 'perfect level' - the creation of an environment in which middle-class men could feel comfortable mixing and playing with those who shared their social sensibilities, unthreatened by others they considered not to be gentlemen – that guided the RFU in the years following the 1895 rugby split. It was this, rather than sporting priorities such as the expansion of the game or success on the playing field, that shaped the RFU's amateurism.

And thanks to its actions in the Edwardian era, the leadership of the RFU got what it wanted: a sport that offered the 'perfect level' upon which middle-class gentlemen could play and socialise among themselves. But reaching that goal had been a difficult and sometimes seemingly contradictory journey. En route the RFU had deliberately sought to restrict the popularity of its game, mercilessly expelled some who were supporters of amateurism and deliberately failed to take action against others who openly violated its amateur code. To paraphrase Oscar Wilde, for whom the year 1895 also proved to be the defining moment of his life, amateurism in rugby union was rarely pure and certainly never simple.

Notes

[1] The original version of this chapter originally appeared as 'The Ambiguities of Amateurism' in Dilwyn Porter and Stephen Wagg's edited book, *Amateurism in British Sport: It Matters Not Who Won or Lost*, published by Routledge in 2007.

[2] For contrasting views of the 1895 split, see Tony Collins, *Rugby's Great Split*, London, 1998, and Eric Dunning and Ken Sheard, *Barbarians, Gentlemen and Players*, Second Edition, London, 2005.

[3] *Yorkshire Post*, 29 Sept. 1897.

[4] RFU annual general meeting minutes, 19 September 1895.

[5] Philip Trevor, *Rugby Union Football*, London, 1922, p. 22.

[6] *Yorkshire Post*, 21 January 1901, *Athletic News*, 17 October 1898, *Yorkshire Post*, 14 April 1902.

[7] *Yorkshire Post*, 20 September 1895.

[8] A.W. Pullin in *Athletic News* 7 Feb, 1898.

[9] Source: RFU *Handbooks* (London), 1895, 1905 and 1910. In contrast the NU numbered 220 clubs in membership in 1905, although by 1910 this had declined to 149; see NRFU *Official Guides* for 1904-05 and 1909-10.

[10] Philip Trevor, 'Football during the Season', p. 431.

[11] David Gallaher and W.T. Stead, *The Complete Rugby Footballer*, London, 1906, p. 222.

[12] *Yorkshire Post*, 13 May 1898.

[13] *Yorkshire Post*, 19 November 1897 and 18 December 1898.

[14] *Yorkshire Post*, 8 February 1902 and 1 September 1902.

[15] *Yorkshire Post*, 30 June and 26 September 1904, 9 January 1905, 31 March 1906.

[16] *Yorkshire Post*, 15 March 1905

[17] For West Hartlepool's financial troubles, see the *Yorkshire Post*, 14 June 1902.

[18] 'An Original All Black' writing in the *Yorkshire Post*, 13 November 1908.

[19] *Yorkshire Post*, 21 September 1900.

[20] RFU AGM minutes, 21 September 1900 and 30 September 1904.

[21] *Yorkshire Post*, 20 February 1896.

[22] For example, see the dispute between Belgrave R.F.C. and Premier Works R.F.C. in Leicester F.C. General Committee minute books, 26 August 1908 (held in Leicestershire County Archives, Leicester, 23D56/1/6)

[23] A detailed account of the report can be found in the *Yorkshire Post*, 3 March 1908.

[24] RFU AGM minutes, 28 May 1908.

[25] Crane letter of resignation is in *Yorkshire Post*, 1 February 1909. RFU AGM minutes, 28 May 1909.

[26] For more on the history of rugby in Coventry see Adrian Smith 'An Oval Ball and a Broken City: Coventry, its People, and its Rugby Team' *The International Journal of the History of Sport*, 11, no. 3 (December 1994), and 'Sport, counterfactual history and rugby's twin codes', *International Journal of the History of Sport*, 21, no. 1 (January 2004).

[27] For more on the Coventry NU club, see *Yorkshire Post*, 28 September, 7 and 13 October, and 1, 3, 13 December 1909; Graham Williams 'Midlands Manoeuvres: A History of Northern Unionism in Coventry', *Code 13*, no. 2 (Dec. 1986).

[28] For more on the Gould affair, see David Smith and Gareth Williams

1895 & All That...

Fields of Praise, Cardiff, 1980, pp. 92-9 and pp. 108-112. Full details of the RFU and IB deliberations can be found in the *Yorkshire Post*, 12 January, 7 February and 3 March 1898. Smith in *The Times*, 18 October 1897.

[29] *Country Life*, 16 January 1898.

[30] See Greg Ryan, *The Contest for Rugby Supremacy: Accounting for the 1905 All Blacks*, Christchurch, 2005.

[31] *Yorkshire Post*, 13 January 1909.

[32] *Yorkshire Post*, 20 February 1909.

[33] Marriott letter reprinted in *Yorkshire Post*, 19 January 1909, RFU and IB decisions in *Yorkshire Post*, 1 and 20 February 1909.

[34] RFU committee minutes, 11 February 1906.

[35] For the tour, see G.T. Vincent, 'Practical Imperialism: The Anglo-Welsh Rugby Tour of New
Zealand, 1908', *International Journal of the History of Sport*,
Vol.15, No.1, 1998.

[36] *Yorkshire Post*, 1 January 1900.

[37] *Yorkshire Post*, 24 October 1900 and 17 May 1906. *Hull Daily Mail*, 15 January 1901.

[38] James Mawson to RFU Committee, 10 May 1904 (RFU archives, Twickenham). *Yorkshire Post*, 25 June 1907, 3 and 13 March 1906.

[39] *Yorkshire Post*, 9 and 24 October 1906, 8 April 1907.

[40] For more on Stoop see James Martens, 'They Stooped to Conquer: Rugby Union Football 1895-1914', *Journal of Sport History*, Volume 20, Number 1, (Spring 1993). Poulton changed his name to Poulton-Palmer in 1913 in order to meet the terms of his inheritance from his uncle, G.W. Palmer.

[41] Samuel Hynes, *The Edwardian Turn of Mind*, Princeton, 1968, p. 6.

[42] EHD Sewell, 'Rugby Football and the Colonial Tours' *Fortnightly Review* vol. 82, 1907, p. 427.

[43] *The Sportsman*, 1 October 1890. *Athletic News*, 17 October 1898.

[44] *Yorkshire Post*, 17 December 1904 and 16 March 1903. *Athletic News* 28 March 1898.

[45] *Yorkshire Post*, 6 February 1909.

[46] *Yorkshire Post*, 3 February 1909.

[47] Occupational statistics taken from U.A. Titley & Ross McWhirter, *Centenary History of the Rugby Football Union*

9

Hidden History:
Black Players in Rugby League

When Clive Sullivan lifted the Rugby League World Cup trophy in Lyons in 1972, he was making history in more ways than many people in rugby league would realise.

Not only was he then, as now, only the third British player to captain a World Cup winning side, but he was also the first black player to captain a major British national sports team. The enormity of this event caused no comment in the rugby league press. But then again, a black man captaining a rugby league team was nothing new in the game.[1]

Few British sports, if any, have a record of racial integration which can compare to that of rugby league.

As early as 1903 a black player, whose name is sadly not recorded, played in the Pendlebury side that won the Lancashire Junior Cup. Black players first played professional rugby league before World War One. They appeared at international level in the 1930s and from the 1960s were such a common sight on rugby league pitches that it ceased to be noticed. In comparison to soccer, the contrast is striking.

Whereas George Bennett became the first black player to appear in international rugby league in 1935, it was fully forty-four years before Viv Anderson became the first black soccer player to play for England. Similarly, although Clive Sullivan first captained the British rugby league side in 1972, it wasn't until 1993 that Paul Ince became the first black player to captain the England soccer team. And no top flight British soccer club appointed a black British manager until Paul Ince's short reign at Blackburn Rovers in 2008, well over half a century after Roy Francis, and many others in his wake, blazed a trail in league.

Ellery Hanley's achievement of becoming the national coach of the Great Britain rugby league side in 1994 is even less likely to be emulated in any of the other football codes. Rugby union in England and Wales was no better than soccer. Aside from the isolated example of James Peters in 1906, no black player appeared in an England rugby union national side until Chris Oti in 1988. Similarly, despite numerous black players appearing in the Welsh national rugby league team, no black player was selected to play for the Welsh rugby union side until the 1980s.

But the history of black rugby league players is both hidden and deeply contradictory.

It is hidden because few writers on the history of black people in British sport are aware of the achievements of black players in rugby league.

For example, Ernest Cashmore's otherwise comprehensive 1982 book *Black Sportsmen* contains no reference to rugby league whatsoever. Contradictory, because league's apparently greater levels of racial integration are shaped and constrained by underlying racist assumptions of British society. This chapter will uncover the hidden history of black players in rugby league while exploring the limits of racial integration in the game.

Race, empire and the 1895 rugby split

Rugby in the nineteenth century was shaped by the Muscular Christian idea that the aim of sport was to educate young men for the greater game of running the British Empire at home and abroad - as the ardent rugby union correspondent of the *Yorkshire Post* said in 1886, rugby's aim was: 'to educate in those important elements which have done so much to make the Anglo-Saxon race the best soldiers, sailors and colonists in the world'.[2]

Conversely, those working-class players and spectators who did not accept the ethos of the Rugby Football Union (RFU), either because they demanded payment for playing or because they jeered and heckled referees and opposing teams, were often viewed in the same light as those subject to British imperial rule overseas: 'I could not expect worse from the heathens of darkest Africa,' claimed J.H. Jones after he had been jeered and booed while refereeing a match at Hull.[3]

These issues came to the fore during the 1888 New Zealand Native tour of the British Isles.[4]

The original intention of the organisers was that the team should be an exclusively Māori side. However, five Pākehā (as the European settlers were known) were eventually selected resulting in the team being called the New Zealand Native Football Representatives. Initially the tour was welcomed in a spirit of colonial reconciliation by the RFU - a generation earlier, the Māori people had fought a bitter and bloody war against the imposition of British rule, only being subdued by a British force of proportionately unprecedented size.[5] As soon as they arrived, the New

Zealanders demonstrated that ability on the rugby field was not the genetic inheritance of English public school boys. Well-organised, powerful and highly skilled, the tourists embarrassed a number of leading British sides, winning forty-nine of their seventy-four matches.

Their success was not appreciated by their hosts, who believed that rugby's hierarchy was being threatened. Joe Warbrick, the organiser of the tour, later summed up the attitude of the RFU: 'as long as [the tourists] were losing they were jolly good fellows in the eyes of the crowd. But as soon as they commenced to win they were hooted and the papers were full of the weakness of the home side and the rough play of the visitors'.[6]

In the latter stages of the tour, a number of leading Southern clubs even turned down the opportunity to play the tourists. The most notorious incident occurred when, during the international match against England, the New Zealanders followed the supposedly gentlemanly ethics of the RFU. England's A.E. Stoddart tore his shorts and the New Zealanders stopped play while he put on a new pair. England's Frank Evershed promptly picked up the ball and scored a try. The referee, RFU secretary Rowland Hill, dismissed New Zealand protests that they were only doing the decent thing and allowed the try to stand. As the tourists departed, *The Field*, sporting magazine of London society, disdainfully referred to 'our dusky brothers' and expressed the hope that Māori players would be excluded from any future New Zealand touring sides.[7]

But in the north of England, where players and spectators were overwhelmingly working class, attitudes differed. While not completely free of the racism expressed by *The Field*, northern crowds welcomed the tourists, appreciating their brand of rugby and identifying with the fact that, like the tourists, they too had suffered at the hands of the social exclusivity of the RFU. More importantly, in the north the game was viewed as a spectacle, as a form of entertainment. The tourists were welcomed for the competition they provided and for the element of the exotic, both of which brought in the crowds. Many northern clubs, flushed with the financial success of their initial matches with the tourists, arranged a second game with them. Northern sports journalists became, in the words of the tourists' manager Thomas Eyton, 'almost members of the Maori Brotherhood'.[8]

It wasn't until 1905 that the RFU hosted another major tour from overseas. But in the intervening period English rugby had been torn apart by the RFU's insistence on pristine amateurism. The very elements which had made the 1888 tourists popular in the north - a shared sense of exclusion and a view of the sport as a commercial spectacle - were central to the Northern Union. In particular, this sense of exclusion was reinforced both by the RFU's ban on NU players and its derogatory portrayal of the NU. For example, former RFU president Arthur Budd described the NU as a 'most admirable drainpipe. A man who would cook accounts would steal your watch, and is capable of any kind of inequity. We are well rid of such persons.'[9]

Such contempt was reciprocated by many supporters of the NU, most remarkably by a correspondent to the *Yorkshire Post* who identified the rebel rugby organisation with the spirit of Huckleberry Finn, the hero of the classic anti-slavery novel: 'I say with Mark Twain's bold, bad boy, that we glory in the sentence of outlawry pronounced on us, as freeing us from the tyrannical bondage of the English union, and we breath pure air in being freed from the stifling atmosphere of deceit in which we previously existed.'[10] Thus from its very inception, the NU defined itself as a sport of the unjustly excluded.

By the time the first New Zealand rugby league tour took place in 1907, such attitudes had hardened, helping to create a distinct sport with its own unique rules and culture. Although race appears to have played no role in the selection of the first Kiwis, the tour brought back memories of the 1888 tour, not least because two of the tourists, W.T. and J.R. Wynyard, were nephews of the three Wynyard brothers on the original tour.[11] Indeed, most journalists saw the 1907 tourists as the continuators of the 1888 side and eagerly regaled readers with stories of their particular club's 'previous meetings with the New Zealanders'. Vilified in their own country and scorned as a 'phantom side' by supporters of the RFU, the 1907 tourists' success helped to cement rugby league's self-image as an open, democratic sport.

In 1912 Hunslet signed the game's first black professional player, Lucius Banks.[12] Banks, a US soldier, was spotted playing American football by a former member of Hunslet's committee living in New York. The club, then challenging for the league championship, bought out Banks from the US Army and he made his rugby league debut on 27 January 1912, scoring a try in a match against York.[13]

Although his presence significantly swelled the attendance at this first game, the welcome was not unanimous. 'Hunslet's Coloured Coon' was the headline in the *Yorkshire Evening Post*, while the generally anti-Northern Union *Yorkshire Post* complained that his selection was unfair to local players and patronisingly suggested that if the club wanted to sign 'coloured' players they should go to South Africa, where 'they are reputed to be capable goal kickers with bare feet.'[14]

Despite this racist opposition, Banks and the club persevered with their attempt to translate his abilities in one football code to another. Playing on the wing he scored four tries in his first three games but the strength of Hunslet's back division limited his opportunities. An attempt to develop him as stand-off was unsuccessful and he faded from the scene in 1913.

That same year, Barrow signed the first black Englishman to play the game professionally, James 'Jimmy' Peters, a dockyard carpenter from Plymouth of West Indian background. Unlike Banks, Peters had a rugby pedigree, having played as a stand-off half for the England rugby union side five times between 1906 and 1908. His selection was highly controversial, one journalist commenting that 'his selection is by no means popular on racial grounds'. In contrast, none of the Barrow newspapers which announced his signing for the rugby league side even mentioned the colour of his skin.[15] In his early thirties when he switched to league, Peters was unable to transfer his rugby union skills and he spent most of his time playing in Barrow's reserve side before moving to St. Helens the following year, where his career was ended by the onset of World War One.

Black players to the fore

By the 1930s, British rugby league had developed a uniquely cosmopolitan flavour, as its traditional base of white northern working class players was supplemented not only by white players from Australia, New Zealand and South Africa but also by Maori and black players. At a time when black boxers where barred from fighting for British championships - despite being prominent in British boxing for well over a century - and other black sportsmen rarely achieved prominence of any sort, still less play at international level, black players began to make their presence felt at the highest levels of rugby league.[16]

Most notable was Wigan stand-off George Bennett, who

signed for the club in 1930 and quickly established a reputation as a skilled playmaker, eventually making 232 appearances for the club and recording over a century of tries. In 1935 he made the first of his three appearances for Wales in their inaugural international match against France. Even more successful internationally was Oldham loose-forward Alec Givvons, who missed only two of Wales's eight matches between 1936 and the outbreak of World War Two. Of particular note is the fact that both played in central, decision-making positions on the field and appear not to have suffered from stereotypical assumptions about black players being suited only for positions based on speed or strength - Givvons later became an 'A' team coach at Oldham and Huddersfield. Even so, this did not stop Bennett being nicknamed 'Darkie' by the press.

It wasn't just in Wales that international pioneers appeared. In 1937 Broughton Rangers' Jimmy Cumberbatch became the first black player to be selected for England when he scored two tries against France at Thrum Hall. His brother Val played for Barrow and he scored a try on his debut for England against France in Paris in 1938. Born in Liverpool, the family moved to Barrow where they both played for the St. Matthews amateur club. In 1936, Val scored six tries in one match for Barrow, a record that is still unbeaten, although equalled, today. Jimmy was the star signing of the short-lived Newcastle team that played from 1936 to 1938. Both Jimmy and Val were viewed as possible selections for the 1936 Lions' tour to Australia but missed out to a stellar collection of all-time great wingers that were playing in the mid-1930s, Stan Brogden, Alan Edwards, Jack Morley and Barney Hudson. When the tourists arrived in Sydney however questions were asked whether racial prejudice had played a role in the brothers' omission from the side, an accusation that was strongly denied.

But perhaps the most prominent black player of the 1930s only began to make an impact in the following decade. Roy Francis signed for Wigan as a seventeen year-old stand-off or winger in 1936. Roy believed that Wigan's manager, Australian Harry Sunderland, did not like the colour of his skin and he was transferred to Barrow after just twelve matches in the first team.[17]

Francis became noted both for his elusiveness and his leadership on the field: he was not only 'a man capable of snatching the vital try at a critical stage, he is also talented at keeping up the morale of his team generally... it is he who, with a choice remark or slight action, can rapidly dispel the tension of a critical moment.'[18]

After making his debut for Wales in March 1946 it was widely expected that he would be named in that year's British side to tour Australia and New Zealand, yet, seemingly inexplicably, he was omitted. It later became widely believed that he was left out of the tour party by the rugby league authorities so as not to offend the Australian government's 'White Australia' policy.[19]

Francis eventually played for the Great Britain side in 1947, two years before he moved to Hull, where he became, as far as we know, the first ever black person to coach a professional sports team in Britain. Brilliant as he was as a player, his achievements as a rugby league coach were even more outstanding. He turned a mediocre Hull side into championship winners - but more than that, he brought to the game motivational techniques, fitness regimes and tactical innovations which were generally unknown to the sport until Australian coaches such as Terry Fearnley and Jack Gibson began studying American football in the late 1960s. Moving to become coach of Leeds in 1963, he enjoyed further success and built one of the all-time great Leeds sides. In 1968 he was appointed head coach of North

Sydney. At a time when Australian rugby league was taking the first steps in a playing and coaching revolution which would take the sport to unprecedented levels, Francis seemed the ideal man to usher in a new age. Instead, he faced a wall of hostility. While many put it down to his being a 'Pom', Australian slang for British, it was animated by racism - *Rugby League Week* even comparing him to Othello and Malcolm X, the courageous American fighter for black liberation, in order to imply that his race made him an unreliable troublemaker.[20] Deeply disillusioned, he returned to England to coach Leeds and later Bradford.

The success of Roy Francis in the 1940s heralded the beginnings of a significant presence of black players in professional rugby league in England. In 1951, Cec Thompson, a second-row forward with Hunslet who had been born in Leeds, became the first black Englishman to be selected for Great Britain when he played against New Zealand. In 1955 he was made captain of Workington Town, where he had transferred in 1953, and in 1960 he was appointed as coach of Barrow.[21]

More famously, in 1953 Wigan signed winger Billy Boston, a man who was to become a local legend.

Boston was such a phenomenon that he was selected for the British tour of Australia a matter of months after making his rugby league debut, becoming the youngest-ever tourist and, on tour, establishing a new record for tries on a tour. He became one of Wigan's greatest players, and his total of 571 career tries, the second highest ever recorded, won him a founder's place in the British Rugby League Hall of Fame. But despite his status, he too was to suffer from racist humiliation, strongly believing that the RFL deliberately left him out of the sides which played exhibition games in South Africa following Australasian tours in 1957 and 1962. In 1962 he was detained by New

Zealand immigration officials when entering the country with the British touring party.

In 1954, winger Johnny Freeman, who went to the same school in Cardiff as Boston, signed for Halifax and eventually became holder of the club record for tries in a career, appearing in a Wales thirteen in 1963. Colin Dixon, a centre three-quarter, followed the same route from South Wales to Halifax in the early sixties, becoming club captain at the age of 23 and making fourteen international appearances in a career which spanned three decades. On retirement as a player, he too become a coach. Of even greater prominence was Clive Sullivan, who was signed by the Hull club in 1961. A winger with a trademark of drifting infield to take advantage of play, he was appointed Great Britain captain in 1972, leading the side to victory in the that year's World Cup Final. He eventually made 22 international appearances, scored career centuries of tries for both Hull clubs and ended his career as coach at Doncaster.

This roll-call of black players achieving at the highest levels of rugby league continued through the 1980s and 1990s.

Des Drummond, Henderson Gill, Roy Powell, Martin Offiah, Phil Ford, Sonny Nickle, Alan Hunte, Carl Gibson and Jason Robinson all appeared for Great Britain, but no player, of whatever race, dominated the British game like Ellery Hanley. Born in Leeds, Hanley rose to prominence as a stand-off in the early 1980s, when he became the first player since Billy Boston to score sixty tries in a season. Transferring to Wigan in 1985, he switched to the loose-forward position and as captain of the side helped steer it to become league's world club champions. In 1987 he was appointed Great Britain captain, a position he held until his retirement from international football in 1992, and in 1995 he became Great Britain coach, the first black person to coach a major British national sports side.

Integration and discrimination

Why is it that rugby league has such a record of integration on the playing field?

As we have seen, from its inception the game found itself excluded from the mainstream of British sport and its self-perception as a democratic sport open to all allowed it to welcome players who would be excluded from other sports or whose opportunities. would be severely restricted. Its emphasis on ability and merit meant that racial barriers did not carry the same weight in the game as they did in other, more socially conservative, sports. As we saw earlier in the use of the quote from *Huckleberry Finn*, many in rugby league were quite conscious, and in some cases proud, of their aberrant position in relation to middle-class sporting norms. Thus it was far easier for a predominantly white sport with such an ideological stance to accept black players in positions of authority.

The commercialism of the sport also obliged it to seek crowd-pleasing players from wherever it could find them. Unlike soccer, its main rival in the north of England, rugby league did not have the national presence to ensure consistently high levels of spectator interest and constantly sought to bolster itself through the importation of overseas players, cup competitions and international tours. Its quest to enhance itself as a spectacle therefore obliged it to ignore many of the social norms governing other sports.

If a player was good enough to attract more paying spectators through the turnstiles, club officials were unlikely to worry about the colour of his skin. Similarly, when appointing coaches, the key criterion was the ability to mould a winning side, regardless of race or other social factors, because that would bring commercial success.

On a broader level, the fact that rugby league existed in an almost entirely separate sphere from the middle and upper-classes meant that it was not wholly part of national public life. In this, it was a cultural expression of what Tom Nairn has described as the working class's consciousness of being 'something of an exile inside the society which [they] supported.'[22]

The game's marginalised position in society was reinforced by the attitudes of its opponents, particularly those in rugby union, who portrayed it as mercenary and morally inferior. Identified exclusively with the industrial working class of northern England, it lacked the social status of other sports, even soccer. To a limited extent, it therefore shared a sense of exclusion from society with those who suffered from racial oppression. This intersection of race and class status was captured by Cec Thompson when he remembered the problems he faced as young man: 'It was bad enough being black... How much lower down the social scale could one go than be seen as a black, uneducated rugby league player..?'[23]

These factors therefore created a recognition that rugby league stood apart from the sporting mainstream and offered a relatively open and meritocratic alternative to those sports more tightly bound to the racist status quo. Such a belief may well have helped to persuade Wally McArthur, the Australian aboriginal sprinter, to sign for Rochdale Hornets in 1953 after he had been left out of the 1952 Australian Olympic athletics squad. Similarly, a small but significant number of black South African rugby union players escaped the iron heel of apartheid by moving to play with English rugby league sides in the 1960s and 1970s, such as Green Vigo and future Great Britain international Dave

Barends. Although it did not come to fruition, possibly the most spectacular example of this openness was Wakefield Trinity's attempt to sign John Carlos, the American 200 metres bronze medalist at the 1968 Olympics whose black power salute on the victory rostrum led to him and Tommie Smith being vindictively banned from international athletics.

But it is the case of black Welsh players which provides the best evidence for the idea that rugby league's aberrant position in society made it attractive to players from racial minorities. Many of them, such as Billy Boston, Johnny Freeman and Colin Dixon, came from the docklands area of Cardiff, home to one of Britain's oldest and largest black communities, and their families had experienced racism at its most stark. In 1919 the community was attacked for two days by rioting white racist mobs.[24] Using the provisions of the Aliens Order of 1920 and the Special Restriction (Coloured Alien Seamen) Order of 1925, the Cardiff police classified all black men as aliens, regardless of place of birth or legal status. In 1935 black seaman were effectively purged from all jobs on the Cardiff docks, forcing the black community into even greater poverty.

In addition to the overt racism experienced off the field, black rugby union players were disadvantaged by the link between the sport and Welsh national identity. As expressed through rugby union, Welsh nationalism was closely tied to British imperial identity: indeed, Welsh rugby was 'profoundly pro-British'.[25] Rather than being separatist or oppositional, it took pride in proving that the Welsh nation was the best representative of the British imperial ideal - which meant that a white skin was a prerequisite for success. Faced with open hostility in their daily lives and institutionalised racism in their sport, there can be little wonder that young black rugby union players eagerly accepted contracts from rugby league clubs in the north of England. The fact that they would be banned for life by the Welsh rugby union authorities was far less of a threat to their future prospects than to those who were white. And by the 1950s and 1960s, the presence of black players at the highest levels of league was a positive incentive for other black players to switch sports - one of the key factors in persuading Clive Sullivan to sign for Hull was the success of Billy Boston.[26] Many black players stayed in the towns where their talents had earned respect and made them a living after their league careers were over. Indeed, Boston and Sullivan became heroes in their adopted homes of Wigan and Hull, developing the same iconic relationship with these towns as that which C.L.R. James described West Indian cricketer Learie Constantine having with the Lancashire town of Nelson.[27]

But the relative openness of rugby league was not simply confined to the north of England. Its ideology was carried with it wherever the game was established. This was particularly true in New Zealand, where it became closely identified with the Maori and Polynesian communities. Especially in Auckland, rugby league has been traditionally the sport of working-class Maori and Polynesian immigrants. The identification of league with the non-white communities of New Zealand has grown stronger over the past two decades, especially with the decline of the mining and associated industries of the west coast where the sport was strong among the area's white working class. It is now common for the New Zealand national team to be composed entirely of Maori and Polynesian players. In Australia, rugby league's position differed from the English and New Zealand games in that it was the dominant sport in the eastern states of New South Wales and Queensland. Moreover, its close relationship with the Australian Labor

Party, a supporter of the long-standing 'White Australia' policy, meant that league was neither subject to the same exclusion from society nor as immediately identifiable with racial minorities who suffered from institutionalised discrimination. Nevertheless, the ostensibly democratic ideological underpinnings of the league game remained a powerful force. Perceived by both itself and wider society as being 'the working man's (sic) game', and drawing its playing strength and supporters overwhelmingly from the working classes, it has, claims Colin Tatz, the historian of aboriginal sport, 'been more generous to aborigines [than other Australian sports]: it has provided easier access, readier acceptance, better facilities, and more encouragement...'[28]

Although this may be an overstatement, it is undeniable that a number of black and aboriginal players made their mark on Australian rugby league as early as the inter-war years. The earliest pioneers were George Green, a hooker, who played for Sydney's Eastern Suburbs side in 1908 and went on to play for and coach North Sydney in the 1920s, and Paul Tranquille, a New South Wales sprint champion, who also played for Norths at the same time. Recent research has suggested that Green and Tranquille were respectively of Afro-Caribbean and Mauritian descent, rather than Aboriginal.[29]

Aboriginal players made appearances for state representative sides in the 1920s and 1930s. Probably the most notable aboriginal player of this period was Lin Johnson, who played twice for New South Wales and kicked the winning goal for Canterbury in the 1942 Sydney Grand Final. His brother Dick also played in the 1939 and 1947 Grand Finals. By the 1970s, following the liberalisation of some aspects of Australia's official racism towards the aboriginal population, Australian rugby league had achieved an apparently high level of racial integration on the playing field. Beginning with Lionel Morgan in 1960, aboriginal players regularly played for the Australian national side, with Arthur Beetson achieving the rare distinction of both captaining and coaching his country, and Mal Meninga, of Solomon Islands descent, making an unprecedented four Australian tours of Britain, twice as captain.[30]

Nevertheless, there remains a great degree of racial segregation in the lower levels of rugby league, where all-aboriginal teams were, and remain, common in local competitions. Such teams have become an expression of racial pride and a means of competing with white people on equal terms, opportunities for which were largely precluded from the daily lives of aboriginal people. Such has been the identification of aboriginal people with the sport that there have been calls to form a professional all-aboriginal team to play in the national Australian rugby league competition. Thus the same open, meritocratic ideology has allowed league to became the sport of choice of another marginalised, racially oppressed group.

The limits of ideology

Faced with such evidence, it is undeniable that, in many ways, rugby league has a unique record of racial integration when compared to other sports. But does that also mean, as others have claimed, that the sport 'remains admirably committed to a radical policy on race and colour' and that 'it has sought to blend together, over the last sixty years, indigenous and immigrant cultures in new and experimental forms'?[31]

This is a claim too far. Rugby league is deeply contradictory, its ideological stance of openness and democracy having definite limits in practice. While it may be excluded from the mainstream of British sport, it is still very much part of British society.

On the field of play, where historically it appears to be far more integrated than other sports, there is incontrovertible evidence that, while black league players may have greater opportunities to rise to prominence in the game, they are restricted by racial prejudice in the positions they occupy on the field. The phenomenon of 'stacking', or positional segregation, has been well documented in studies of American professional baseball and football, and, to a lesser extent, in English soccer and Australian rugby league.[32]

All of these studies found that black players largely occupied non-central, non-decision making positions - for example, few black players played in the quarterback role in American football or in the critical midfield positions in soccer. In particular, these studies noted that black players were confined to positions which required speed and strength, and conformed to racially stereotyped notions about black people being 'natural athletes', 'fast runners' and so on.

Similar conclusions can be drawn about British rugby league. In the years 1984 to 1994 the Great Britain rugby league side, made up of the best English, Welsh and occasionally Scottish players, played sixty-five games, in which thirteen black players made an aggregate total of 152 appearances. In only one game during that time was there no black player in the side. Despite this representation, over 68 per cent of the appearances made by black players were in the wing or centre positions, traditionally those roles in which speed is the most important factor. Even more tellingly, not a single black player appeared for the national side in the two critical playmaking positions of scrum-half and hooker. Of the other positions, all of the stand-off half and loose forward appearances were made by one man, Ellery Hanley, and, of the other twelve black players, only Phil Ford at full-back, Roy Powell at prop and Sonny Nickle at second-row forward appeared in any position other than winger or centre. Similar findings were reported at club level by Long *et al*, who discovered in their study of racism in professional club rugby league that of thirty-eight black players in English divisions one and two, twenty-four were wingers, fully 63 per cent of the total. This also conforms to the pattern found in Australian rugby league, where Hallinan found that almost 60 per cent of aboriginal players played in the positions of winger or centre.[33]

Such positional segregation has historically been the norm. By and large, the vast majority of black players who have become famous in league have been wingers. Similar stereotyping can also be seen in the fact that, of black players coming to prominence in the forward positions, most of them have played as second-row forwards, traditionally seen as a role requiring speed and strength. That such stereotypical views run deep within the sport was highlighted by the remarks of Barry Maranta, owner of the London Broncos rugby league side, when he announced in 1995 that his club was going to target its player recruitment drive on local black youths: 'They can't play soccer because of their size, but... they're Wendell Sailors [Brisbane Broncos' star black winger/second-row forward]. They can sit on the wing and bust through tackles.'[34]

As this statement demonstrates, rugby league does not share English soccer's widespread racist belief that black players lack physical courage or, to use the vernacular, that they 'do not have the bottle'. Nevertheless, the sport's emphasis on the speed and strength of black players fits perfectly with prevailing racial stereotypes.[35]

Off the field, there is little evidence to suggest that the

sport poses a conscious challenge to prevailing attitudes on race. Throughout the 1950s, there were constant accusations from senior figures in the game, such as Eddie Waring and Gus Risman, that racism on the part of the selectors was responsible for keeping Cec Thompson out of the British side.[36]

More recently, in 1988 Des Drummond was left out of the British touring party to Australia and New Zealand after defending himself from a supporter who rushed on to the pitch shouting racist abuse. Racial abuse of players by crowds has been commonplace, although not on the widespread and horrific scale of English soccer. Even in the 1950s, Billy Boston, a seemingly universally popular player, was subject to such taunting, as Eddie Waring noted: 'there were many matches in England when Boston had to stand up to crowd comments about his play and colour - and more than once he went towards the crowd.' Long *et al*'s study of racism in rugby league in the mid-1990s noted that racial abuse of black players by supporters was 'a small but significant problem'.[37]

The crowds at rugby league matches have remained overwhelmingly white. Significantly, Long *et al* discovered that, on the date of their survey, there were more black people, thirty-eight, playing professional rugby league than were watching it, who totalled just twenty-four. Despite the success of black players in the sport, there appears to be little incentive for black people to become supporters. Rugby league's continuing lack of status means that it is not perceived as a method of social integration, unlike in Australia where the sport has been seen as a route to integration by immigrant communities.

More to the point, league is perceived by black and Asian communities as being an exclusively white sport - for example, when noted black British author Caryl Philips made a radio programme about race and sport in the 1980s, he made no mention of rugby league, despite the fact that he was raised in Leeds.[38] This perception reflects the reality both of the racial composition of league crowds but also the lack of relationship of the sport with its local minority communities.

These factors are most graphically highlighted by rugby league's relationship, or lack of it, with its local Asian community.

In the early 1960s many Asians emigrated from the Indian sub-continent to take jobs in the textiles mills of the north of England, traditionally a key industrial base of rugby league support. By the 1970s, large numbers of rugby league clubs found themselves in towns and cities with significant Asian populations; some, such as Halifax and Keighley, found that the working class housing areas surrounding their stadia had become the centres of local Asian communities. However, the sport has done little to attract Asian players or spectators to the game.

In contrast to the success of players with an Afro-Caribbean background, only two Asian players, the brothers Ikram and Tony Butt, have played professional rugby league - Ikram Butt playing for England in 1995 - and only three others, Safraz Patel, Gurjinderpal Pahal and Junaid Malik, have received representative honours in amateur rugby league, the first two as youth internationals.

Just as racist stereotypes have helped to segregate black players in peripheral positions in league, stereotypes about Asian people not being physically strong, despite the popularity of wrestling and Kabaddi in Asian communities, are used to explain the lack of Asian participation in the game.

The close proximity of many rugby league clubs to Asian communities only serves to emphasise - by way of contrast -

the huge gulf between the sport's ideological rhetoric and the reality of the limited degree of integration it offers.

Conclusion

Rugby league is therefore deeply contradictory. An unrivalled history of achievement by black players and coaches coexists with deep-rooted racial stereotyping and estrangement from local minority communities. How can these seemingly mutually contradictory factors inhabit the same sport?

The key to understanding rugby league's relationship to racial minorities lies in the importance of commercialism to the game. It was the clash between the amateur ideology of the rugby union authorities and the commercial necessities of rugby in the North of England which led to the 1895 split and the creation of rugby league. The combination of exclusion from the British sporting mainstream and the need to provide a spectacle to attract paying spectators allowed league to develop an ideology more meritocratic and open than other mass spectator sports. In a very real sense therefore, rugby league provided players of all races a chance to take advantage of the 'equality of the balance sheet'.

But this equality was open only to those who could help the sport fulfil its commercial needs. Thus the vast majority of black players in league before the 1970s came from outside of the traditional rugby league-playing regions and had already established sufficiently high reputations to increase spectator interest in the clubs for which they signed.

The sport therefore saw no need to combat racial stereotyping in the game or racist assumptions among its almost entirely white following - what it desired was players who would help its clubs become successful, regardless of race but also regardless of any need to oppose racism. This also explains why it has done little to encourage the participation of local black and Asian communities in the sport: the effort required to stimulate interest in these communities is not viewed as being cost-effective, not to mention an unwillingness to do so because of the prevalence of racist attitudes to non-white communities within the game.

The fact that its star black players were usually from outside of its localities also allowed the game to step aside from confronting the problems of racism in its own regions.

The ambiguous history of rugby league must also throw doubt on the widespread belief that sport can somehow be a force in helping to overcome racism in society.

As we have seen, even a sport with league's ideological predisposition to identify with those facing discrimination is largely incapable of confronting deeper aspects of racial stereotyping and institutionalised discrimination. Moreover, it may well be the case that league's apparently successful record of on-field integration serves as a self-congratulatory barrier to it confronting its inability to break out of its traditional white working class constituency and build support among its local black and Asian communities.

In short, rugby league demonstrates that having a significant number of black players in prominent positions does not mean that a sport is either free of racism or that it represents a clear alternative to sports more overtly committed to racist policies.

Nevertheless, as a sport which was marginalised in its relation to British national identity and society, rugby league offered an opportunity to excel in sport to those who also felt themselves marginalised by society and had been denied such opportunities by other sports. But, driven by commercial necessity, the game was also a product of that society and reflected, albeit in different forms, its racism - the chains which shackled black people in other sports had not been cut by rugby league, merely loosened.

Notes

[1] The original version of this chapter was written in 1997 and published as 'Racial Minorities in a Marginalised Sport: Race, Discrimination and Integration in Rugby League', *Immigrants and Minorities*, Vol. 17, No. 1 (March 1998). Since then the story of black and minority league players has been expanded in a book I edited with Phil Melling, *The Glory of Their Times*, Skipton, 2004.

[2] *Yorkshire Post* 29 November 1886.

[3] *Yorkshire Post* 21 February 1893.

[4] For full details of the tour see Greg Ryan, *Forerunners of the All Blacks*, Canterbury, 1993.

[5] For a comprehensive account of the New Zealand Wars see James Belich, *The New Zealand Wars and the Victorian Interpretation of Racial Conflict*, Auckland, 1986. At the height of the war, the British had 18,000 troops in place to oppose a total Maori population of just 60,000.

[6] Quoted in Ryan, p. 94.

[7] *The Field*, 30 March 1889.

[8] Quoted in Ryan, p. 91.

[9] Arthur Budd, 'The Past Season' in *Athletic News Football Annual 1897*, Manchester, 1897, p. 194.

[10] *Yorkshire Post*, 21 September 1895.

[11] W.T. Wynyard was also to become the founding treasurer of the New Zealand Rugby League, and another brother, G.A., was also a founding member of the NZRL executive committee.

[12] *Yorkshire Post*, 29 January 1912.

[13] In the process, Banks also became the first American to play rugby league and probably only the fourth black American to play professional football of any code. Only three black American footballers had played professionally up to 1912: see Mike Rathet and Don R Smith, 'We're here to play football' in Richard Whittingham (ed.) *The Fireside Book of Pro Football*, New York, 1989.

[14] *Yorkshire Evening Post*, 26 January 1912. *Yorkshire Post,* 29 January 1912.

[15] *Yorkshire Post*, 17 March 1906. For details of Peters' signing for Barrow

rugby league club, see *Barrow News*, 11 October and 29 November 1913 and the *North West Daily Mail,* 6 October 1913.

[16] For black boxers, see Peter Fryer, *Staying Power: The History of Black People in Britain*, London, 1984. Only one black athlete represented Britain at the Olympics during this period, sprinter Jack London in 1928. Although evidence is at best sparse, it appears that very few black players appeared for professional soccer sides in England before World War Two: three of the most notable being Arthur Wharton, a former sprinter who played as goalkeeper for Preston North End in the 1880s; Walter Tull, who signed for Tottenham Hotspur in 1909; and Jack Leslie, who made over 350 appearances for Plymouth Argyle in the 1920s.

[17] See Robert Gate's obituary to Roy Francis in *Code 13*, issue 11, June 1989, p. 4

[18] 'Airlie Robin' quoted in Robert Gate, *Gone North*, Vol. 1, Ripponden, 1986, p. 50.

[19] Despite strenuously looking for evidence I have found nothing to confirm the truth of this belief. Even Under the White Australia policy, the Australian authorities did allow non-white athletes to compete in the country, the most famous example being the boxer Jack Johnson in 1908.

[20] Andrew Moore, *The Mighty Bears! A Social History of North Sydney*, Sydney, 1996, pp.214-26.

[21] Cec Thompson, *Born on the Wrong Side*, Durham, 1995.

[22] Tom Nairn, 'The English Working Class', in Robin Blackburn (ed.), *Ideology in Social Science*, London, 1972, p. 198.

[23] Cec Thompson, *Born On The Wrong Side*, London 1995, p. 27.

[24] See Neil Evans, 'The South Wales race riots of 1919', *Llafur*, Vol. 3, No. 1, Spring 1980, Ron Ramdin, *The Making of the Black Working Class in Britain*, Aldershot, 1987.

[25] David Smith, 'People's Theatre: A Century of Welsh Rugby', *History Today*, March 1981.

[26] Joe Latus, *Hard Road To The Top*, Hull, 1973, p. 35.

[27] For C.L.R. James on Constantine, see *Beyond A Boundary*, London, 1963, p. 127.

[28] Colin Tatz, *Aborigines in Sport*, Adelaide, 1987, p. 80.

[29] Much of the detail here is taken from Colin Tatz, *Obstacle Race: Aborigines in Sport*, Sydney, 1995. Andrew Moore has researched the backgrounds of Green and Tranquille in *The Mighty Bears!*, chapter two.

[30] Colin Tatz, *Aborigines in Sport*, p. 83.

[31] Phil Melling, 'Definitions for the Definers, not the Defined', *The Sports Historian*, No. 16, May 1996, p. 29.

[32] J.W. Loy and J.W. McElvogue, 'Racial Segregation in American Sport', *International Review for the Sociology of Sport*, 5.25 (1970). J.A. Maguire, "Race' and Position Assignment in English Soccer: A Preliminary Analysis of Ethnicity and Sport in Britain', *Sociology of Sport Journal*, 5, 3, (1988). C.J. Hallinan, 'Aborigines and positional segregation in Australian rugby league', *International Review for the Sociology of Sport*, 26.2 (1991).

[33] J. Long, N. Tongue, K. Spracklen and B. Carrington, *What's The Difference? A study of the nature and extent of racism in rugby league*, Leeds Metropolitan University, 1995. For Australia, see Hallinan, pp. 74-5.

[34] Barry Maranta, quoted in *Rugby League Express*, 28 April 1995.

[35] On racism in English soccer, see Dave Hill, *Out Of His Skin: the John Barnes Phenomenon*, London, 1989.

[36] Cec Thompson, *Born On The Wrong Side*, pp. 29 and 34.

[37] Eddie Waring, *The Great Ones*, London, 1969, p. 95.

[38] Caryl Phillips, 'Can Sport Break Down Racial Prejudice?' *The Listener*, 24 May 1984.

10

'Ahr Waggy':
Harold Wagstaff & The Making of
Anglo-Australian Rugby League Culture

I would like to start by saying what an honour it is to be invited to give this year's Tom Brock Memorial lecture.[1] Among the small band of rugby league historians in Britain Tom was a well-known and highly respected figure - so I hope that in some small way this lecture is in the way of being a tribute to the help and encouragement he provided to British historians over the years.

Certainly I hope I'm more successful than other recent British rugby league visitors to Sydney - I note with trepidation that it's almost a year to the day since the pride of Great Britain flew into Sydney to take on Australia; only to fly straight back out again on the back of a 64-10 defeat.

In such circumstances it seems downright perverse to ask a Pom to come and talk to an Australian audience about rugby league. In fact the only thing I can think of which would be even more perverse would be to ask a Pom to come over to talk about cricket.

It's usual at events like this for the speaker to start with a few comments about his or her journey. Well, in the mental geography of the British rugby league supporter, the journey to Sydney is not very far at all; it's just a little bit further east than Hull.

Most kids growing up in a rugby league environment in Britain will know the suburbs of Sydney better than those of London. Growing up in Hull in the late 1960s, I could point out Penrith and North Sydney on a map of Sydney but I'd be hard-pressed to show you where Surbiton or Twickenham were on a map of London.

I remember when I was maybe nine or ten, every Friday afternoon at school the teacher would give a pop quiz; she'd pick a letter and ask for the name of an animal, vegetable, country, town etc that began with that letter. One day she picked 'P'; when she asked for a town I said Parramatta. 'I've never heard of that, where is it?' she asked. 'In Australia' I replied. 'Are you sure you're not making it up?' she said. At that point one of my mates, a fellow Hull KR supporter stuck his hand up and said 'Please Miss, I've heard of Parramatta'. I'd like to be able to report that, just like in the movie *Spartacus*, all the kids rose one by one to declare that they too had heard of Parramatta. Sadly, they didn't, but the fact that at least three of us in the class had heard of it demonstrated what journalist Adrian MacGregor has described as the 'intangible bond' between rugby league in the two countries.

Which is what I want to talk about tonight. I want to look at how Anglo-Australian rugby league culture was formed, the parallels between the sport in the two countries and why the link has proved so durable. And I want to do that by looking at the career of possibly the greatest English league player of all, Harold Wagstaff.

Why Wagstaff? Wagstaff is crucial to cementing the link

between Britain and Australia. He captained the 1914 and 1920 British touring teams to Australia and New Zealand, tours which established the template for future tours and he led Huddersfield's 'Empire Team of All The Talents', a side which heavily featured Australian stars as it swept all before it in the years immediately before World War One, in the process helping to establish the tradition of Australian players in the English league. Just as importantly, he played a central role in the three key developments in rugby league that helped to forge a shared culture and identity for the sport in the two countries in the second decade of the twentieth century; namely, the development of a trade unionist, oppositional outlook among players, an innate sense of superiority over rugby union, and the contradictory combination of a working-class democratic spirit with loyalty to the Empire. On top of the shared social circumstances of the rugby splits of 1895 and 1907-8, these developments helped to solidify Anglo-Australian rugby league culture.

Wagstaff's greatness was recognised by English and Australians alike. North Sydney's Sid Deane argued that Wagstaff was the difference between the two sides in the 1914 Ashes series: 'Harold Wagstaff was not only brilliant in attack and wonderful in defence but his leadership was a most important factor in the team's success.' Dinny Campbell of Easts and later Norths described him as ' the greatest tactician I ever played against. His personality was dynamic.' *The Referee's* football correspondent, JC Davies, wrote about the 1914 third Test, the so-called 'Rorke's Drift' Test, that 'Wagstaff, always a great player, that day became *the ubiquitous*, and the King of the game … Here, there and everywhere, all the time he was doing the work of half-a-dozen men. Wagstaff the Great.' In 1946, seven years after his early death, the Sydney *Rugby League News* gave pride of place to Wagstaff's memoir of the 1914 series as part of its build-up to that year's Test series.

As can be seen from these quotes, there is something totemic about Wagstaff, in his achievements, his reputation, almost in his very being. Even his name is quintessentially northern English. He was always Harold, not Harry with its connotations of princes of the English realm. The name almost seems to have be designed to emphasise the flat vowel sounds of Yorkshire and Lancashire. And of course the aitch was rarely sounded - he was 'Arold, not Harold - a signifier of working-class speech in both the north and south of England.

His nickname too, 'Ahr Waggy', underlines the close and familial relationship he had with the game's supporters; in the north to prefix someone's name with 'Our' denotes a close family member, conveying, in the words of Richard Hoggart, a 'sense of connection, of being part of a larger possessive whole, of not being only discrete individuals'. In this, he parallels Gracie Fields, the singing star of the 1930s who hailed from Rochdale, and was known universally as 'Our Gracie'. (Incidentally, I'm informed by John O'Hara that in Australia this honour was extended only to 'Our Don' Bradman and the singer 'Our Glad[ys]' Moncrieff.)

'I am a Northern Union man all the way through,' Wagstaff declared in the first sentence of a series of autobiographical articles published in 1934, 'and I was suckled in the Northern Union game'. He never played any other form of football seriously and did not even see a game of rugby union until he was in Australia on the 1914 British tour. He was born in 1891 in Holmfirth, a village now familiar to anyone who has ever seen the long-running BBC TV series *Last of the Summer Wine*. He made his debut for the local amateur side, Underbank Rangers, aged fourteen and the following season scored their first try under the new thirteen-a-side, play the ball rules in September 1906. Two months later he signed as a professional for Huddersfield, aged fifteen years and 175 days, the youngest ever. Two years later he made his debut in representative football for Yorkshire, selected to some extent because of his policy of not kicking the ball, a practise he continued to preach throughout his career, which eventually led to Huddersfield becoming known as the team which wouldn't kick, parallelling the great Souths sides down the years. A few weeks later he made his England debut against the 1908 Kangaroos. Eighteen months later, aged just nineteen he was appointed captain of Huddersfield, a post he was to hold for the next fifteen years. Aged twenty-two, he was made captain of the national side.

The blossoming of his career matched that of the Huddersfield side. Crucial to that success were its Australian stars such as Glebe's Tommy Gleason, Newcastle's Paddy Walsh and, most of all, Easts great Albert Rosenfeld, who scored over 200 tries in just three seasons, Wagstaff's team finished top of the Championship table every season between 1911 and 1915, won the Challenge Cup twice and the Yorkshire Cup three times. In the 1914-15 season they won every trophy available to them, losing only two games in the entire season.

They played the game in fast, open style that made the fullest use of the opportunities provided by the NU's rules, developing new tactics - such as 'scientific obstruction', the 'standing pass' and a hostility to kicking the ball - which moved the game far beyond the static set-pieces of its origins. It was no accident that the metaphors and adjectives most commonly used to describe the team were those of science and industry, as exemplified by a 1924 description of the side:

There was an absolute understanding between all parts of a perfectly working machine which resulted in the most audacious and unexpected movements being carried out with a precision that left the opposing defence aghast. Fast and clever three-quarters were served by halves whose brains were ever working at high pressure behind forwards who, as occasion demanded, could play the traditional scrummaging game or convert themselves into temporary three-quarters and handle the ball.

For a town which had been built on the efficiency of its textiles mills and spectators whose day-to-day lives were based on synchronised, collective working in those mills, Wagstaff's team was the embodiment of working-class industrial collectivity at play.

However, despite this iconic status and the high regard in which he was universally held, it is important to note that Wagstaff did not have an unproblematic relationship with the rugby league authorities, even after his retirement as a player. Indeed, the same can be said of many of Wagstaff's peers in the rugby league pantheon - of the nine players inducted into British rugby league's Hall of Fame in 1988, only the two Australians did not at some point clash with either their clubs or the RFL itself. This antagonism between players and officials came to a head shortly after the outbreak of World War One.

There has been a good deal of work produced in Australia on the war and the two rugby codes, such as that of Chris Cuneen and Murray Phillips. What is less widely known is that a similar, but not exact, division took place in England; union ceased operations in September 1914 while league carried on, although only unofficial competitions took place after 1915. More importantly, in November 1914, three months after the declaration of war, English rugby league was hit by a series of players' strikes opposing wage cuts which had been proposed by the clubs. Referees too threatened to go on strike. The players were led by a four man committee, comprising Wagstaff, Gwyn Thomas, a Welsh full-back from Wigan who later joined Huddersfield, Charlie Seeling, the veteran NZ and Wigan player who had toured Britain with both the 1905 union and the 1907 league All Blacks, and Leeds's Australian centre-threequarter, Dinny Campbell. The fact that the four leaders came from England, Australia, New Zealand and Wales - emphasising the international character of the sport in England - was also, consciously or not, highly symbolic.

Faced with a threat of all-out strike action, the Rugby League authorities caved in and the compulsory wage cuts were rescinded. It is important to understand the context of these strikes - in the early months of the war there had been a huge hue and cry against professional football by large sections of the national press, much of it led by Rugby Union supporters, who believed that those who played or watched professional football were failing in their patriotic duty to volunteer for the army. To go on strike for their rights as professional footballers was significantly out of step with the militarist hysteria which seemingly prevailed in Britain. Although there is no evidence of players explicitly opposing the war, their failure to completely fall in line illustrates the fact that pro-war hysteria was by no means the norm among sections of the British working-class. It is interesting to note that the majority of league players only joined the armed forces after conscription was introduced through the back door in early 1916. And indeed a recent study of the town of Huddersfield during the war has discovered deep levels of indifference and hostility to the war effort.

The so-called 'national unity' of World War One did not extinguish oppositional attitudes among players. In November 1920 Wagstaff and Gwyn Thomas were the two central figures in the formation of the Players' Union, the initiative for which had been generated on the 1920 British tour to Australia. For much of the next eighteen months the RFL spent considerable time attempting to head-off the union's demands for higher wages, better benefits for players and a more equitable transfer system. The union's formation reflected the tremendous surge in class conflict which took place in Britain in the years following the end of the war.

During this time Salford, Oldham, Barrow, Hull and Halifax all had to deal with threatened or actual strikes by players, and the union itself threatened two national players' strikes, although on both occasions it found itself out-manoeuvred by the RFL. But by the end of 1922 the inexperience of the union's leadership, coupled with Wagstaff's health problems with a stomach ulcer and Thomas's somewhat abrupt flight to America, not to mention the divide and rule tactics of the clubs, led to the end of the Players' Union. However, it wasn't the last time that Wagstaff was to clash with the RFL - in 1929 he was initially refused permission to sit on the Huddersfield club committee because he was a former professional player.

Although British rugby league never had the same close links with the Labour Party that the Australian game had, the attitude towards the war and the deep divisions after it demonstrate a similarity of oppositional outlook that was shared among wide sections of both the Australian and British working classes. What's more, the cultural antagonism towards the southern English middle-class archetype was also shared, in spades, by the northern English working classes.

This was most obviously demonstrated by the attitude shown towards the rugby union game by rugby league in both countries. Following the recruitment of most of the leading rugby league players into the armed forces in 1916, services union sides began grabbing them like kids in a candy store. The first significant match took place in April 1916 at Leeds when Wagstaff and three other league tourists were picked for a 'North of England Military XV' against an ANZACs XV, featuring Australians Tommy Gleason, Newtown's Viv Farnsworth and Norths' Jimmy Devereux and Sid Deane. Despite never having played the game and seeing only one union match in his life, Wagstaff was the star of the match.

Later that year, Wagstaff, Albert Rosenfeld and half a dozen other league stars mysteriously found themselves all assigned to the same Army Motor Transport depot at Grove Park in South London, whose commanding officer just happened to be a member of the RFU executive committee. During the 1916-17 season the Grove Park union team tore apart almost every other team in the south of England, including Australian and New Zealand services sides, winning 25 out of 26 games and scoring 1110 points while conceding just 41, setting a new British union record for points in a season. Their only defeat was a last minute 6-3 loss to a United Services side which included eight rugby union internationals plus Wigan's Billy Seddon and Leeds' Willie Davies. There was no secret to their success; as Wagstaff described it, the Grove Park team simply played 'rugby league football under rugby union rules'.

The record of the Grove Park team in the war, and to a lesser extent that of the similar Royal Navy Devonport side, firmly ended any lingering sense of inferiority rugby league supporters may have had in relation to union. In the eyes of rugby league and the communities in which it was based, rugby union, as in Australia, was quite clearly the junior code, less skilful, less athletic and much less satisfying for players and spectators alike. This sense of superiority was underlined in the north of England by use of the everyday phrase 'best in the Northern Union', the implication being that if it was the best in the Northern Union, it was also better than anything else.

So, overlaid on top of the objective similarities in class and social circumstances of rugby league players in Britain and Australia, British players had also gone through experiences as club employees, as players in war-time and in rugby union which had given rise to attitudes and an outlook very similar to that Australian players. Wagstaff himself noted that players of the two countries were noticeably more friendly - off the pitch, of course - following World War One. It is also interesting to contrast the relations between Australian and British league players with those in the union game. The 1908 Wallabies were shocked at the level of snobbery they encountered and until the 1980s the British rugby union press had little positive to say about Australian players and tactics. Even as late as 1998, one of the reasons given for the sacking of Bob Dwyer as Leicester rugby union coach was the fact that he was 'too Australian'.

This could not be more different to league. Many Australian players who played for English rugby league clubs remained there after they had stopped playing. Albert Rosenfeld who came over with the first Australian tourists in 1908, lived in Huddersfield until he died in 1970, working for most of his life as a dustman. The peerless winger Brian Bevan has a statue erected to his memory in Warrington. Arthur Clues, who made his reputation through ferocious assaults on the 1946 British tourists, settled in Leeds, becoming probably the most prominent of its sporting celebrities. When he died in 1998, the church had to close its doors because so many people wanted to go his funeral. A similar point can be made about many of the British players who came to play in Australia in the 1960s and 1970s and stayed on, such as Dick Huddart, Dave Bolton and Tommy Bishop.

This shared common identity could be seen as surprising given the ferocity and violence which were an integral part of Ashes Test matches. The tone was set by the 1914 'Rorke's Drift' third Test match - in which the two sets of players slugged it out to such an extent that at one point the British were down to nine players, yet still managed to pull off an amazing 14-6 victory, despite a second half which lasted 54 minutes due to stoppages for injuries. Six years later, the first Test match between the two countries following the First World War set the tone for what was to come: 'the contest was not characterised by anything striking in sportsmanship: that is, the striking things done were with fists or boots,' wrote one reporter This intensified even more in the 1930s. The 1932 tour became notorious for the second Test match, the 'Battle of Brisbane', which Australia won despite being reduced to ten men at one point because of the injuries, and both the first Test and the match against the Queensland representative side were also characterised by fierce violence. Journalist Claude Corbett described the Brisbane match as 'hard all the time, rough most of the time and foul frequently'.

Nor did the experience of the Second World War do much to halt the violence; less than half an hour into the first Test match following the war, Bradford school teacher Jack Kitching was sent off for punching Australian captain Joe Jorgensen. Clive Churchill's abiding memory of the 1948 Kangaroo tour to Britain was the violence of the English club sides. Most notoriously the 1954 Britain versus New South Wales tour match was abandoned by the referee just sixteen minutes into the second half due to fighting. And the 1960s saw more players sent off in Test matches than in any other decade.

Yet such behaviour was never once used as a reason to question, let alone break, the relationship between the Australian and British rugby league authorities. This stands in marked contrast to the Bodyline cricket tour of 1932-33 when Jardine's bowling tactics appeared to threaten the future of Anglo-Australian cricket. Far worse misdemeanours than Jardine's were committed by British league players a few months before Jardine's men arrived in Australia without a hint of an international incident. Partly this can be explained by the importance of cricket to the Empire and the upper classes of society. Yet, the 1932 Test series created massive interest in Australia, being watched by almost 150,000 people, and press coverage, especially for the 'Battle of Brisbane' Test, often moved from the back to the front pages of the newspapers. The opportunity certainly existed for at least the more sensationalist sections of the press to question the relationship between the two countries' rugby league authorities.

But this did not happen, due to two interconnected and contradictory reasons. Firstly, as we have seen, because of the deep cultural affinities between the predominantly working-class constituency of the sport in the two countries. Secondly, and perhaps more controversially, the fact that Australian rugby league officials were as fundamentally loyal to the Empire as were their British counterparts.

In passing, I would argue that these were the reasons which also scuppered the 1914 and 1933 talks between the NSWRL and the VFL which discussed the possibility of forming a united nationwide Australian football code. The discussions came to nothing, partly because of differences over the rules but also, I would suggest, because a united game couldn't offer this combination of working-class self-assertion and the imperial link.

The leaders of Australian league were extremely vigorous in their belief in Britishness. Harry Sunderland told the 1928 tourists to 'remember Captain Cook; if he hadn't planted the Union Jack here, Australia might have become a Dutch dependency'. 'We are just as British as you are,' explained Harry 'Jersey' Flegg, the president of the New South Wales Rugby League, in 1950 during a dispute with British tour manager George Oldroyd. 'Australians look to England as the mother country in war, in industry and also in rugby league football,' said Kangaroo tour manager E. S. Brown in an address to the RFL Council in 1954, pointing out that 'there is a strong desire in Australia to get along with England from every point of view'. When H. V. Evatt met the leaders of British rugby league in 1945, he argued that a tour to Australasia by the British was vital for 'the best interests of rugby league football and of the Empire'.

Just as importantly, it was the Australian press, far more than the British, which utilised imperial imagery for league Test matches. It was they who dubbed the 1914 third Test in Sydney as 'the Rorke's Drift Test', in comparison with the 1879 battle of Rorke's Drift during the Anglo-Zulu war, when 100 British troops held off 3,000 Zulu warriors. In parentheses, it must be noted that a book published this year, *Zulu Victory* by Ron Lock and Peter Quantrill reveals that the British forces who relieved the troops at Rorke's Drift also massacred over 800 wounded Zulu prisoners in the aftermath. The battle of Rorke's Drift appears to have had special significance for Sydney; in 1882 the Art Gallery of New South Wales purchased Alphonse de Neuville's painting 'The Defence of Rorke's Drift', which you can still see prominently displayed in the gallery today. The use of such rhetoric continued even as late as 1958 when *Truth* began its report of the second Test, again a landmark British victory against overwhelming odds, by quoting Shakespeare: 'This happy breed of men, this little world ... this England.' Examples such as this, I would argue, also raise questions about the strength of Australian nationalism as expressed through sport before the 1960s.

But this loyalty to the Empire was also tempered with a hostility to many of the social mores of British society, especially its deference and class snobbery. Whereas Jardine, and English cricket captains in general until the late 1960s, were the embodiment of the English Imperial elite, rugby league players manifestly were not. British rugby league tourists were not seen as representatives of a distant, and perhaps alien, government. In fact, they had far more in common with Australia's self-image as a country of the (white) working man than with the privilege and class discrimination that English cricket represented. Much of the hostility towards Australia from the British upper- and middle-classes was based on a social snobbery which was also directed with equal venom at the working-class in Britain - 'an entire continent peopled by the Lower Orders' in the words of English upper-class novelist Angela Thirkell. Jardine's tactics were unacceptable to Australians to a great extent because of what he represented. Yet physical intimidation and worse by a British rugby league side that shared the same social background and suffered similar frustrations as the great mass of Australians was a 'fair dinkum' part of the game.

Rugby league perfectly encapsulated the two seemingly contradictory attitudes of imperial loyalty but hostility to privilege. And Anglo-Australian Test matches provided the arena in which both aspects of this relationship could be demonstrated. For many Australians and working-class

Britons, the British rugby league tourists presented an image of the Empire in their own self-proclaimed likeness: working-class, democratic and meritocratic. Made up of workers from the industrial heartlands of Britain the British players were men just as they were. This sense of shared identity was sometimes reflected by the combatants on the field: when Nat Silcock and Ray Stehr were sent off for fighting in the first Test match of 1936, they shook hands once they had left the field. During the 1958 Brisbane Test Australian captain Brian Davies forbade his players from attacking British captain Alan Prescott's broken right arm (although this decision was heavily criticised by Clive Churchill among others). Most tellingly, following the 1954 abandoned match Britain versus New South Wales match, the players met that night at a dance and, according to Clive Churchill, 'had a good laugh' about the match - although Aub Oxford, who sadly died a few weeks ago, the referee who had abandoned the match, never refereed at that level again.

This leads to my final and perhaps the most important point about the significance of Harold Wagstaff to Anglo-Australian rugby league culture. Touring British rugby league sides were exclusively working-class - almost uniquely in comparison to any other sports' touring sides such as cricket or rugby union - and were captained and led by men who by and large worked with their hands when not playing football.

In an age when working people did not travel around the world - unless they were soldiers, sailors or emigrants, and then it was always under the command of their so-called social superiors - it was almost unheard of for a working-class person to hold such a leadership position (outside of the labour movement). At best, a working-class man - and the situation for working-class women was far worse - could hope to be a trusted servant or the stereotypically loyal 'Tommy Atkins' character.

For working-class Australians, just as much as British, to see an working-class man such as Wagstaff as a leader of a British national side was an almost unprecedented event, which, along with his football skills, perhaps explains the tremendous coverage Wagstaff was given in the Australian press.

Wagstaff stood out as a symbol of what working people could achieve given the opportunity to get a 'fair go'. And it was rugby league which gave him, and many others from similar backgrounds, that opportunity. In the British army he would have been a NCO at best, but in rugby league he was a five star general. In short, he became 'Ahr Waggy' not just for English rugby league followers but for Australians too.

Wagstaff's memoirs of the 1914 Rorke's Drift Test match were reprinted as much in Australia as they were in Britain - in 1946 the Sydney *Rugby League News* gave them centre stage in its preview of the first Ashes Test following World War Two, and as late as 1992 they were prominently featured in Geoff Armstrong's *The Greatest Game* compendium. One of the interesting points about the 1946 coverage is that discourse on the tour was wrapped up with the idea that rugby league was the most democratic of sports, as can be seen in this example from the *Rugby League News*. This was also repeated in Britain - the strength of the democratic ideal in league was (and is) very strong, beginning with the rationale for the split in 1895. British journalist Eddie Waring was a regular proponent of this view, and it was this sense that rugby league represented something more than merely sport which accounts for the fury of rugby league supporters around the world against Rupert Murdoch's attempt to takeover the game in the 1990s.

I would like to end on a partisan note; after all, this is a lecture to honour a great supporter of rugby league and I have been proud to call myself a rugby league supporter since I was seven years old. The great Jewish novelist Isaac Bashevis Singer once noted that Yiddish had never been the language of a ruling class. A similar point can be made about rugby league: it has never been the sport of a ruling class in any of the countries in which it is played. Some see that as its weakness - on the contrary, that is precisely from where its strength is drawn. For without its deep roots in the working-classes of the north of England and eastern Australia, the game would have survived neither the persecution of the rugby union authorities nor the corporate attacks of the Murdoch empire (nor, incidentally, its banning by the Nazi collaborators of France's war-time Vichy government).

It is this working-class, democratic, 'battler' spirit - which is central to the sport in both Britain and Australia, and which is embodied in the career of Harold Wagstaff - that, to use a phrase that I believe that would be endorsed by Wagstaff, Tom Brock and countless others across Australia and Britain, has helped to make rugby league the greatest game of all.

Notes

[1] This is the transcript of the talk I gave for the 2003 Tom Brock Lecture, an annual lecture held in Sydney in memory of rugby league historian and South Sydney supporter Tom Brock.

Record breaker - Huddersfield's Albert Rosenfeld

11

From Bondi to Batley:
Australian Players in British Rugby League

Hardly a day goes by today without the question of overseas players being discussed in one sport or another. In Britain, the huge influx of overseas players into soccer's Premier League and the widespread importation of players into English rugby union over the past ten years has highlighted the extent to which sport now has a global labour market. But the transfer of players across nations and continents is not a new phenomenon. British rugby league has always sought to recruit players from beyond its geographical confines.[1]

Because rugby league is a marginalised sport in British society and commercially driven by the need to attract spectators, it has historically viewed as a global labour market all of those countries in which it is played, and also to a lesser extent those in which rugby union is played too.

The most obvious example is the hundreds of Welsh rugby union players who have 'gone north' since the 1880s to benefit financially from their rugby skills. In this migration from the Celtic nations to England's industrial heartland, rugby league was not unique. Thousands of Scottish soccer players took their talents south over the years to earn greater rewards than they could gain at home.[2]

But what has made British rugby league different from other sports is the fact that from 1908, when the first Australian rugby league touring side arrived in Britain, over 1,500 Australians have trekked halfway around the world to find football fame and fortune in the north of England. In doing so, they have provided British rugby league, often thought of as geographically insular and parochial, with a cosmopolitanism which was, until recent times, unique in British sport.

Many of their exploits have been recorded in Dave Hadfield's 1992 book *Playing Away*.[3] This chapter looks the ways in which Australian players have helped to shape and define the culture of British rugby league - and also how those returning home influenced Australian rugby league. It places the importation of Australian players in the context of the changing balance of power between the British and Australian games, and looks at the questions of national identity and the shared working-class culture of rugby league.

1907-1937: Pioneers

Of A.H. Baskerville's pioneering 1907 professional All-Black New Zealand tourists to Britain, six went on to play for British clubs, including Lance Todd, whose name lives on in the trophy for the Wembley Challenge Cup Final player of the match. When the first Kangaroos arrived from Australia the following year, ten players, or almost a third of the tour party, signed for English clubs.

The great Huddersfield 'team of empire talents' that won twelve out of a possible sixteen trophies between 1911 and 1915 period had two Australians. One of them was Albert Rosenfeld, who scored what was thought to be a never-to-be-beaten record of seventy-eight tries in a season in 1912, only to better it two seasons later with a phenomenal eighty tries. Oldham signed three of the first Kangaroos who then helped the club to two rugby league championships in 1910 and 1911. By 1912 they were one of three English clubs with Australian captains, two others having New Zealanders in charge. The Hull side which won the 1914 Challenge Cup had Jimmy Devereux and Steve Darmody directing the side.

In the six years between the initial Australian tour and the outbreak of World War One, only two sides without an Australian in a key position won the RL championship. One of those was Wigan, runners-up on four consecutive occasions, who had built their success on a combination of New Zealanders and Welshmen. Such was the strength of the Australian and New Zealand presence in the British game that a combined Australia/New Zealand 'Colonial' team thrashed the returning British tourists 31-15 in September 1910.

The impact of the 'Colonials' was not just on the playing field. As well as increased credibility from tours to and from Down Under, the Northern Union gained a uniquely cosmopolitan flavour - the importation of overseas players into the game gave the NU its own alternative to the glamour of soccer's nation-wide competitions and the social cachet of rugby union. This, together with the move to thirteen-a-side and the introduction of the orderly play-the-ball in 1906, was crucial in creating the template for modern rugby league.

By the beginning of the 1909-10 season the *Yorkshire Post* estimated that there were at least twenty 'Colonial' players playing in Britain. Unsurprisingly, the administrators of the fledgling Australian and New Zealand rugby leagues were not pleased with what many saw as the looting of some of their best players. In November 1909 the British authorities acceded to their requests and introduced the first regulations governing player transfers between the hemispheres. Any player wishing to sign for an English club now had to have the permission of his home league and club.[4] Those without it had to serve a two-year residency period before playing - which, in effect, meant that international transfers were banned. A revolt of British clubs at the start of 1912 led the NU to cancel the ban but furious threats from Australia forced its reimposition in February 1912.

Following World War One, British clubs again tried to remove the ban. The RFL succumbed to this pressure in the summer of 1923, only to re-instate the restrictions a few weeks later after protests from Australia.[5] This time the ban was extended to include rugby union players from Australia and New Zealand. However, by 1927 the British clubs' desire to boost their attendances through antipodean glamour proved too strong and in June of that year they forced the removal of the restrictions on international transfers.

This marked the beginning of a new golden age, providing a temporary respite from the gloom of the depression years for the mining villages, mill towns and industrial cities across Yorkshire and Lancashire. Ernest Mills and Ray Markham at Huddersfield, Vic Hey, Eric Harris and Jeff Moores at Leeds, Hector Gee at Wigan - a departure from their then traditional policy of signing New Zealanders - and Bill Shankland at Warrington, were merely the most prominent of the Australians who lit up the football fields of northern England in the 1930s. Significant earnings

were available to these players: Bill Shankland was paid a
£1,000 signing-on fee plus £6 per match and given a job
paying £8 a week.[6] But not all were successful. Dave Brown,
one of Australia's greatest ever players, never made his
mark at Warrington, and Kangaroo half-back Joe 'Chimpy'
Busch, 'scorer' of the most famous non-try in rugby league
history when his touchdown in the 1930 third Ashes Test
match was controversially disallowed, also failed to fulfil his
potential at Leeds.

Although the acquisition of such stars delighted English
spectators it brought no pleasure to Australian rugby league,
nor, for that matter, to those in the English game who feared
its detrimental effect on international competition. To
assuage these fears, the RFL agreed in 1931 to compensation
of £200 per player to be paid by British clubs to the
Australian or New Zealand authorities. But by the mid-
1930s the extent of the player drain meant that it was
becoming commonplace for journalists to wonder if
Australia would ever beat Britain in a Test series. Once
signed to an English club, a player's contractual obligations
and the difficulty of international travel meant that they
were no longer eligible for international selection. The
precedent had been set following the attempt of Dan
Frawley, the 1908 Kangaroo, to play for the 1911 tourists
despite being contracted to Warrington. The club refused to
let him to play for Australia, but his contract was sufficiently
ambiguous to allow him to eventually play later in the tour.
Henceforth British clubs made sure that there was no
ambiguity: a player's responsibility was first and foremost
to his club. This meant that Eric Harris, the 'Toowoomba
Ghost' who played for Leeds from 1930 to 1940, never got
the chance to play for his country. Indeed, it would have
been quite possible to select an Australian Test side from
those playing for English clubs in the 1930s.

1945-1983: Reversal of Fortunes

To safeguard the competitiveness of international football, the ban was reimposed in 1937 and the flow of players dried up. However, the agreement lapsed in the midst of World War Two and no attention was paid to it until a letter arrived at RFL headquarters in early 1946 from the New Zealand Rugby League, complaining that Wigan had breached the agreement by signing the Ponsonby winger Brian Nordgren. Although the British authorities somewhat cynically dismissed the complaint because neither New Zealand nor Australia had requested a new agreement, they were sufficiently concerned to instruct the two managers of the 1946 British touring side to Australasia to discuss the matter when they arrived down under.[7]

Part of this desire to reach an understanding may have been motivated by rumours that the British tourists would themselves be targets for Australian clubs. In fact, a number were approached when they arrived but none were tempted. For example, Wakefield Trinity forward Harry Murphy was offered £300 to sign for Balmain plus a three year contract paying £9 per match. He turned it down because, as the Wakefield secretary explained, 'He was brought up on the Trinity ground. He has been with us since he was sixteen and in his job as a marine engineer he has prospects which will develop as he grows older.'[8]

Balmain's terms were barely more than what Murphy received at Wakefield and offered little incentive to move. Although more prominent players were probably offered more money, it is unlikely that Australian clubs had the finances to match the wages offered by English clubs. The growth in British crowds after World War Two offered the prospect of higher wages and post-war economic reconstruction appeared to promise long-term employment opportunities. And, as implied by the above quote, British insularity probably also played a role in players' reluctance to move. In his study of migrant soccer players in Colombia in 1950, Tony Mason noted that 'British players put up the strongest cultural resistance to life in a foreign land', bolstered by the prevailing belief that 'British is Best.'[9]

The opportunities offered by a resurgent British game did not go unnoticed by Australian players nor unpublicised by scouts acting for British clubs. The international transfer ban was not renewed until the beginning of the 1947-48 season, which gave a vital window of opportunity to British clubs to take their pick of Antipodean talent. If the 1930s were a golden age for overseas players, the players signed in 1946 and 1947 helped raise the British game to even greater heights, among them being Brian Bevan, Harry Bath, Arthur Clues, Lionel Cooper, Pat Devery, and Johnny Hunter.

Possibly even more than the preceding two generations of Australian exiles, this group indelibly marked the sport with a resonance that remains today. Bevan became the most prolific try-scorer ever, with 796. Hunter, Devery and Lionel Cooper especially became the crucial triumvirate in Huddersfield success of the early 1950s. Arthur Clues and a complete three-quarter line of fellow Australians raised Leeds back to the heights they had conquered under their previous generation of imports. The Australians of this era became identified with the huge boom in post-war rugby league attendances.

The influx also had an impact, unappreciated at the time, which was to have a major influence of the future development of the sport. As many of the stars returned to Australia in the late 1950s, they took back new approaches to the game. Future Australian national coach Harry Bath left Warrington to play for St. George in 1957 and was shocked at the poor skills of his new team-mates: 'I couldn't believe the bash and barge way Saints played the game. Blokes knocking themselves stupid. I thought 'Christ! This isn't for me'.'

Dick Huddart, the British international second-row forward who moved to St. George in the 1960s, credits Bath with revolutionising Australian forward play: 'before Harry showed them how to play, Australian forwards were called pigs, and that's how they played. ... all they'd do was put their heads down, get tackled and die with the ball. Harry taught them that there was much more to forward play than that'. Rex Mossop, later to play with Manly, also acknowledged how much his skills improved during his time with Leigh.[10]

Much of the success of St. George's record breaking eleven-premierships between 1956 and 1966 was due to the influence of British playing methods learned by Bath and captain-coach Ken Kearney, who played for Leeds between 1948 and 1952. According to Larry Writer, the highly organised and brutally effective defence of St. George was based on the straight defensive line which many British sides employed at that time. By the mid-1960s, these methods had helped to raise the Australian game to the level of the traditionally dominant British.

In 1947, faced with a new exodus of star players, the Australian Rugby League Board of Control successfully insisted that the ban on unauthorised transfers was re-introduced.[11] But this did not stop English clubs pursuing Australians. Disaster almost struck Australia in 1949 when Workington Town announced they had secured the signature of the South Sydney and Australian full-back Clive Churchill for £12,500 - unsurprisingly, the Australian authorities refused to sanction the move. Writing in the September 1947 issue of *Rugby League Review* Alfred

Drewery said he had little sympathy with the Australian authorities but 'those who look upon rugby league football from an international point of view cannot help but be perturbed at this wholesale drain on Australian talent.'

Undeterred by the ban, British clubs soon realised that it did not apply to rugby union players. Rochdale Hornets hit upon the idea of persuading league players to switch temporarily to rugby union, thus becoming free to transfer to England. In 1950 Rochdale managed to sign five junior players from Newtown, Eastern Suburbs and Albury using this subterfuge until the Australian Board of Control found out and appealed to the RFL to stop Rochdale's undercover operation, complaining that:

> agents scour our junior ranks for players of promise and approach them to sign contracts for English clubs which they represent. If the prospect is interested, these agents advise the lads to forsake rugby league and transfer to rugby union (sometimes under fictitious names). After playing a few matches in rugby union these players are then signed up for English clubs under the guise of being rugby union players.[12]

British scouts also turned their attentions to bona-fide Australian union players such as Wallaby captain Trevor Allen and future league TV commentator Rex Mossop, both of whom signed for Leigh at this time. As Trevor Delaney notes, this proved highly unpopular with league players in Australia who saw their own opportunities to sign lucrative English contracts disappear while those with no league background were free to cash in.[13]

In 1951 it was agreed that all overseas signings, whether

from league or union, had to be sanctioned by the player's domestic rugby league authorities. Finding all doors locked, British clubs' focus for overseas signings turned to South Africa - as had happened in the 1920s - and, to a lesser extent, Fiji.

By the mid-1960s rugby league's international balance of power was perceptibly shifting towards Australia. This was reflected both on the playing field – the 1963 Kangaroo tourists had demolished the British, scoring an unprecedented fifty points in the second Test match at Swinton – and financially too. The legalisation of poker machines in New South Wales in 1956 opened up extensive sources of revenue for clubs. Coupled with the abandonment of the residential qualification for players in 1959 and the development of a formal contract system, Sydney rugby league clubs were now able to match the financial benefits of playing in England.[14]

On a broader level, the imperial relationship between Britain and Australia was also unravelling. Up until the formation of the Rugby League International Board in 1948, the RFL's international authority had been based in large part on the fact it was the representative of the mother country of the British Empire. This was not simply due to British arrogance. As we shall see in chapter thirteen, the Australian authorities themselves were keen to emphasise their loyalty to the Crown.[15] But by the 1960s, Australian society had begun to question such deferential attitudes and this new self-confidence was reflected in Australian rugby league - the British game was no longer regarded as being inherently superior and, for example, coaches began to look to American football for inspiration.

At the same time, British rugby league was sinking into a malaise. Crowds had slumped and the traditional industries from which the game had historically drawn its support, such as mining and textiles, were in acute decline. This was also the era of the 'Ten Pound Poms'. Thanks to the encouragement of the Australian government's Assisted Passage Scheme, emigration to Australia from Britain had become, if not exactly commonplace, a well-used option for those seeking better life and employment prospects in the 1950s and 1960s. For cash-strapped British rugby league clubs, the possibility of large transfer fees from Australian clubs for British players was highly attractive and the RFL consequently gave permission to transfer to a steady stream of British players who had declared their intention to emigrate.

In 1960 Phil Jackson, the Barrow centre who had starred on the 1958 British tour of Australia, accepted an offer to become captain-coach of the Goulburn Workers club. He thus became the first British player of the modern era to move down under to play; the only previous example was Huddersfield's Welsh forward Ben Gronow who moved to Grenfell in New South Wales in 1925 as their coach but returned two years later.[16] In 1963 Derek Hallas moved from Leeds to Parramatta and, over the next decade and a half a series of leading British players made their way down under.

The rugby boot was now firmly on the other foot. If the Australian game had suffered in the past because its talents were being siphoned by British clubs, the reverse was now true. Britain lost almost an entire Test team to Sydney clubs in the 1960s and 1970s. Dick Huddart to St. George, Dave Bolton to Balmain, Malcolm Reilly and Phil Lowe to Manly, Roger Millward, Cliff Watson and Tommy Bishop to Cronulla and John Gray to North Sydney were some of the players who became league stars in both hemispheres. British league was becoming seriously weakened at international level and the 1977 World Cup, in which Great

Britain was forced to field a drastically understrength side due to the loss of numerous leading players to Sydney clubs, was the final straw for the RFL, who successfully lobbied for a new international transfer ban.

1983-1995: The Deluge

Although the British touring team had suffered unprecedented losses in Australia in 1979, it was the historic Kangaroo tour of 1982 which highlighted just how far the domestic game had fallen behind Australia. The shock at the scale of the defeat was traumatic and, desperate to learn as much as possible from their conquerors, the RFL called for an end to the transfer ban. In September 1983, all restrictions on international transfers were lifted... and the floodgates opened.

In the following ten years, 757 Australian players came to play for British clubs.[17] In the first two seasons clubs were free to sign as many players as they wanted: Halifax owner David Brook took this at face value and signed thirteen Australians. This led to a situation in early 1985 when Halifax played Leeds and fielded ten Australian players while Leeds fielded five, with another as a substitute. Many of those that played, often on short-term contracts, became local icons: Mal Meninga at St. Helens, Peter Sterling at Hull, Brett Kenny and John Ferguson at Wigan. Wally Lewis played ten games for Wakefield Trinity and earned additional immortality by being enshrined in the name of the club's fanzine, *Wally Lewis is Coming*.

It goes without saying that many of those signed were not in the class of such exalted company and the rush to sign an Australian player, any Australian player!, seemed to be best exemplified by Runcorn's signing of the world's only one-armed rugby league player, Kerry Gibson. Although this was widely seen as something of a joke signing, Gibson was in fact an accomplished player, having played in reserve grade for Sydney's Western Suburbs in 1983 and 1984. For the players, the primary motivation for coming to Britain was the lucrative contracts available – at the top end Wally Lewis was paid £1,000 per game – and, occasionally, to serve out bans handed down by the NSW Rugby League judiciary, a facility enjoyed by Mario Fenech, Steve Roach and Mark Geyer before the loophole was closed. In an attempt to nip in the bud the growing reliance of some British clubs on their imports, not to mention their increasing financial burden, the RFL introduced a quota of five Australians per club in 1985, reducing it to four in 1986 and three in 1987.

Reaction to the influx of Australian players was marked by two divergent views. The new players were undoubtedly popular with spectators while others within the British game were more sanguine. Unsurprisingly, wholesale importation became the source of dissatisfaction among British players. Halifax's purchase of almost an entire team and the sacking of popular coach Colin Dixon to make way for Canterbury winger Chris Anderson caused considerable dissension, resulting in the enforced transfer of players' spokesman John Carroll. Hull half-back Kevin Harkin retired from the game in disgust after the club signed Peter Sterling and Wally Lewis recounts how only half of his new team mates shook his hand when he arrived at Wakefield Trinity. There were also complaints from Australian players that their British colleagues were often quite happy to let them do more than their fair share of tackling, something which, if Rex Mossop is to be believed, was also common in the 1950s.[18]

But there was more at stake than new players. The traditional British view of the game was being challenged. Unlike the three previous periods of Australian immigration, when the game down under was undeniably the junior partner, players were coming to Britain as representatives of the dominant power in world rugby league. This was perceived by many, especially British coaches, to be a threat to their authority, best expressed by former national coaches Alex Murphy and Peter Fox, who continued to argue for the superiority of the British game, despite its obvious inferiority on the pitch. 'The conventional wisdom in this country is that the Australians play the game at great speed but are stereotyped and lack skill in the finer points of the game,' was how *Open Rugby* summed up this attitude in 1983.[19]

As this passage suggests, national stereotypes came rapidly to the fore: the Australians were all brawn but no brain, whereas the British were perhaps not as athletic but possessed the more cerebral arts of the game. This was a reversion to British beliefs about the game in the 1940s and 1950s, which in the 1980s amounted to little more than wilful blindness. Some even insisted that it was an absence of patriotism which undermined British rugby league: 'players in Great Britain have lost pride for their British shirt', was how former Great Britain and Penrith hooker turned TV commentator Mike Stephenson explained the dominance of the Australians.[20]

In contrast, others wholeheartedly supported the Aussie invasion. Ironically, it was Halifax coach Colin Dixon, who was shortly to find himself dumped to make way for Chris Anderson, who summed up the attitude when he stated that 'English rugby league must look to the future and now the future is Australia'.[21]

Phil Larder, the RFL's newly appointed coaching director, not only met Australian coaches but also conferred with Australian players in Britain about what the British game could learn from them. Among many supporters, a cult of all things Australian developed - like Sidney and Beatrice Webb's view of Stalin's Russia in the 1930s, Australian rugby league represented 'a new civilisation'. A minor industry sprang up importing Australian rugby league videos, books, magazines and playing kit. Kangaroo jerseys were worn by British supporters in the same way that Brazil shirts are worn today by soccer fans. By the late 1980s it was a sign of an enlightened high rugby league fashion sense to wear an Australian replica club shirt to matches.

Did the large number of Australian players bring success to the clubs using them? If we measure success by the winning of the Championship or the Challenge Cup, the sport's two major prizes, the evidence would suggest not. In the ten years following the lifting of transfer restrictions only eighteen Australians appeared for sides winning the Championship, and seven of those played for Halifax in the 1985-86 season. Of the ten sides that won the Challenge Cup in the same period, five of them fielded a total of ten Australians, six of whom played for, yet again, Halifax in 1987. It is also worth noting that Halifax's success was quickly followed by near bankruptcy, relegation to Division Two of the RFL Championship and the departure of the architect of the club's Australian policy, David Brook. In fact, it was New Zealanders who were far more prominent in Championship winning sides and it was they who provided the backbone for Wigan's long dominance of the game from the late 1980s - just as they did for the club's rise to prominence in the era immediately preceding World War One.

Wigan's one long-term Australian acquisition was their Australian coach John Monie. At the start of the 1984-85 season, Monie's predecessor at Parramatta, Jack Gibson, had suggested that British clubs should recruit Australian coaches rather than players.[22] This began to happen in the late 1980s, with Monie being the most prominent, along with Chris Anderson at Halifax and Brian Smith at Hull. It was Monie who built the side which won both the Championship and the Challenge Cup for seven consecutive seasons, in the process becoming the first man ever to coach championship winning sides in Britain and Australia. He was the most successful of the twenty-four Australian coaches who moved to the British game in the late eighties and early nineties. In hindsight, it may well be the case that it is the importation of Australian coaches rather than players that contributed more to the changing face of British rugby league during the 1990s.

Conclusion

The impact of Australian players on British rugby league was such that it is almost impossible to exaggerate their influence. Two of the original nine members of the Rugby Football League's (RFL) Hall of Fame are Australian. Until the dislocation of the 1995-97 'Super League War' the rhythm of its life revolved around the cycle of tours to and from Australia. The history of the British game and its most successful clubs cannot be written without mentioning the role which Australian players have played in it. Australian players brought a glamour and style to the game which helped it transcend its geographical limitations. A successful Australian player in a local side represented an affirmation of the sport's strength and relevance beyond its immediate locality, in defiance of the scorn of the establishment game of rugby union and the threat of the commercial juggernaut of soccer. In the 1980s, the importation of players and coaches provided a reservoir of knowledge and expertise which helped to improve the domestic game.

From an Australian perspective, it is clear that the loss of some of its finest players to British clubs in the 1930s and 1940s seriously undermined its ability to compete successfully with Britain at an international level up to the 1960s.

Yet, paradoxically, the experiences which Australian players in Britain in the 1950s brought back home helped lay the foundations for the eventual eclipse of the British game. In doing so, they contributed to the weakening of the imperial link with Britain in the sporting arena. From being the dominant power in world rugby league, the British have not won an Ashes Test series since 1970 - indeed, the decline in competitiveness of the British national side has led to the New South Wales versus Queensland 'State of Origin' series becoming the pinnacle of the sport internationally and to a growth of insularity in the Australian game. Nowhere was the decline in the strength of British rugby league so clear than when it was used as a mere bargaining chip by Rupert Murdoch's News Corporation against the Australian Rugby League in 1995.

The life of an Australian player in Britain until the 1980s differed little from his British team mate. Both were subject to the same contract and transfer system, although, given his higher profile, the Australian would generally receive higher wages and a higher signing-on bonus. Until the advent of short-term contracts during the Australian off-season in the 1980s, the major difference in their terms of employment was their inability to play for their national team. This led to situations where British players could be chosen to play for Britain in an Ashes Test match yet an Australian playing for the same club could not play for Australia. The iniquity of such a situation was only brought home to the British in the 1970s, when they regularly played Test matches in Australia without their best players, unable to play because of their contractual obligations to their Australian club employers. In contrast to rugby union or cricket - where players from other countries of the British Empire regularly turned out for British national sides - there were never any attempts to 'naturalise' Australian players in order to allow them to play for Britain.

When in the early 1990s former Illawarra hooker Phil Mackenzie, then playing for Widnes, married a British woman, took out British citizenship and declared his desire to play for Britain, it became an open secret that the then British coach Malcolm Reilly would never pick him because he was 'really' an Australian. Indeed, the only exceptions to this rule have been the South African born Dave Barends, in 1979, and the Samoan Maurie Fa'asavalu, in 2007.[23i]

Nevertheless, for many Australian players playing in the north of England, the strands of national, local and self-identity became inextricably interwoven. Many settled in the towns that had welcomed and made them a focus for civic pride. While it is unlikely that they went as 'native' as Rex Mossop claimed of Harry Bath (when Mossop made his debut for Leigh against Warrington, Bath allegedly told his Warrington forwards to 'Get this convict Australian bastard Mossop!') those that chose to stay slipped easily into the culture of the north of England.[24]

Albert Rosenfeld, scorer of an unsurpassable eighty tries in the 1913-14 season, stayed in Huddersfield until he died in 1970, working for most of his life as a dustman. Arthur Clues too stayed on in Leeds, becoming probably the most prominent of its sporting celebrities. When he died in 1998, the church had to close its doors, such were the numbers wishing to attend his funeral. Brian Bevan has a statue erected to his memory in Warrington. As Jeff Hill has also argued in relation to overseas cricket professionals in the 1930s, the Australian rugby league star 'was respected as a man who somehow carried the reputation of the local community on his shoulders'.[25]

The esteem in which Australian players were held by the communities which adopted them was almost without exception reciprocated. No biography of an Australian player who spent time with an British club is complete without a comment about those who watched them play. In a reversal of national stereotypes, Steve Roach found British fans less reserved than Australians. Ken Thornett, who played for Leeds in the early 1960s, encouraged fellow players to get out and meet them. Even players who, like Brett Kenny, had little liking for the British way of life, praised the British supporters. Rex Mossop's comments about Leigh in the 1950s are also representative of the view of the players of the 1980s: 'I loved these loyal supporters, the way they'd cheer and sing at matches and shout you a pint in their cosy, friendly pubs. They made you feel part of a community.'[26] A similar observation was made in 1990 by Australian journalist Adrian MacGregor:

> To east coast Australians, Yorkshire and Lancashire towns are more relevant to their education than the Tower of London. England and Australia have cricket in common but nobody pretends that singular game, by its very nature, possesses the camaraderie of rugby league. It may sound naïve to refer to an international brotherhood of rugby league, yet hundreds of Australians have come to England to play, many to stay. I found that, in the North, to be Australian was to be welcomed, to be an Australian on the rugby league trail ensured a hospitality bred of an intangible bond.'[27]

This 'intangible bond' had its roots in the cultural meanings attached to rugby league.

Although the wheels of commercialism and the lure of hard cash transported Australian players to Britain, it was the culture of the game which made them feel part of a community. As with all sports, that culture reflected the society which nurtured the game. Both the working-classes of the north of England and Australia faced the contempt of imperial rulers in southern England and responded by developing a culture which was ostensibly more democratic, at least for white-skinned people, than that of the London-centred establishment. Rugby league, forged in opposition to the social exclusiveness of rugby union and bolstered by its own self-image as 'the working man's game', embodies some of these common elements of British and Australian working class culture. It was this that enabled British rugby league to welcome Australian players and, in doing so, to act as a bridge linking the sun-kissed beach of Bondi with the dark satanic mills of Batley.

Notes

[1] This chapter was written in 1998 and is based on 'From Bondi to Batley: Australians in British rugby league' *Sporting Traditions*, vol. 16, no. 2, May 2000, pp. 71-86.

[2] See Robert Gate, *Gone North* (two volumes), Ripponden, 1985 and 1986 and Gareth Williams 'The Road to Wigan Pier Revisited: The Migration of Welsh Rugby Talent Since 1918' in John Bale and Joseph Maguire (eds), *The Global Sports Arena*, London, 1994.

[3] See Dave Hadfield, *Playing Away. Australians in British Rugby League*, London, 1992. This article deliberately concludes at 1995, before the outbreak of war between Rupert Murdoch's Super League, supported by the RFL, and the Australian Rugby League, which irrevocably altered the relationships within in national and international rugby league.

[4] Northern Rugby Football Union, General Committee minutes, 9 November 1909.

[5] Rugby Football League, Special General Meeting minutes, 12 July 1923.

[6] Bill Shankland, interviewed by Dave Hadfield in *Playing Away*, p. 26.

[7] Northern Rugby Football League Council minutes, 23 January and 18 March 1946.

[8] *Yorkshire Post*, 30 July 1946.

[9] Tony Mason, 'The Bogota Affair' in Bale and Maguire, p. 47.

[10] Larry Writer, *Never Before, Never Again*, Sydney, 1995, pp. 36-7. Rex Mossop with Larry Writer, *The Moose That Roared*, Randwick NSW, 1991, p. 80.

[11] RFL Council minutes 7 August 1947.

[12] Letter from JK Sharp, secretary of Australian Board of Control, to RFL, 7 July 1950 (copy in RFL Archives, Leeds).

[13] Trevor Delaney, 'A History of Rugby League International Transfer Restrictions', *Code 13*, no. 7, June 1988, p. 26.

[14] For the impact of poker machines on Australian rugby league, see Andrew Moore, *The Mighty Bears*, Sydney 1996, pp. 290-8. For the end of the residential qualification, see Ian Heads, *True Blue*, Randwick, 1992, pp. 298-9.

[15] RFL Council Minutes, 10 October 1945.

[16] See Stanley Chadwick, *Claret & Gold*, The Author, Huddersfield, 1947, p. 45. Phil Jackson's entertaining memoirs were published by Keith Nutter in *Phil Jackson: A Prince Among Centres*, Barrow, 2005. Tom McCabe, the 1908 Kangaroo tourist, played for Widnes before moving to Australia but his decision to emigrate was not rugby-related.

[17] Source: *Rothman's Rugby League Yearbook* Queen Anne Press, London, 1982-83 to 1994-95.

[18] *Shopacheck's Rugby League Review*, Kingswood, London, 1985, p. 84. Peter Sterling with Ian Heads, *Sterlo! Portrait of a Champion*, Sydney, 1989, p. 99. Adrian MacGregor, *King Wally*, St. Lucia, 1987, pp. 149-51. Mossop, p. 77.

[19] *Open Rugby*, October 1983, p. 31.

[20] *The Sun*, 3 November 1982.

[21] *Daily Telegraph*, 3 November 1982.

[22] *Open Rugby*, August 1984, p21.

[23] Tulson Tollett, who was brought up in Australia, was selected for the 1997 British touring side to New Zealand, although he was born in Hastings before his parents emigrated.

[24] Mossop, p. 74.

[25] Jeff Hill, 'Cricket and the Imperial Connection: Overseas Players in Lancashire in the Inter-War Years' in Bale and Maguire, p. 56.
[26] Steve Roach with Ray Chesterton, *Doing My Block*, Randwick, 1992, p. 77. Ken Thornett with Tom Easton, *Tackling Rugby*, Melbourne 1966, p. 21. Brett Kenny in *Open Rugby*, October 1985. Mossop, p. 83.
[27] Adrian MacGregor, *Simply The Best: The 1990 Kangaroos*, St. Lucia, 1991, p. 2.

12

Merger Most Foul: The Australian Rules/ Rugby League Merger Proposal of 1933

In the winter of 1933 the Australian sports' scene was presented with perhaps its most dramatic proposal ever: that rugby league football and Australian Rules football should merge together to form what was to be known as the Universal Football League.[1]

Revealed on the front page of the Sydney sports weekly, the *Referee*, the aim would be to develop 'one common code of football for Australia', that would be to the Australian winter what cricket was to its summer.[2]

Coming just months after the Bodyline tour of Douglas Jardine's English cricket team had seemingly driven a wedge between the two leading sporting nations of the British Empire, the merger seemed to point the way to a football code that was in origin and in geography wholly Australian.

The idea had been mooted in early July 1933 by Horrie Miller, secretary of the New South Wales Rugby League (NSWRL). He had been in Melbourne to see the departure of the fifth Australian Kangaroos touring team to Britain and had travelled back to Sydney with Con Hickey, secretary of both the Australian National Football Council (ANFC) and the Victorian Football League (VFL). Hickey was going north for the eighth Australian National Football Carnival, which was being held for only the second time in Sydney in August, and on the journey north Miller had apparently suggested that they explore the possibilities for a merged game.

As announced to the press, the road to the new merged game was surprisingly simple. A conference was to be held between the NSWRL and the ANFC during August 1933 to coincide with the Sydney Australian Rules carnival. Featuring representative sides from all Australian states, the carnival was seen by the ANFC as a major evangelical event in the previously barren territory of league-dominated Sydney.

But now it appeared that the carnival could be a harbinger of much more important events. The NSWRL/ANFC conference would, it was envisaged, be the start of a process whereby rule changes would be gradually adopted by each sport to bring them into line with each other. The immediate aim of the meeting would be to formulate, in the words of Hickey,

> a proposal of devising ways and means of an
> amalgamation ... by adoption of a common code
> of laws of the game to operate throughout
> Australia, and eventually the world,
> incorporating the best features of the rugby
> league code and the Australian.[3]

To emphasise the joint nature of the initiative, Miller underlined Hickey's sentiments and went on to state that the ultimate goal of the conference would be to establish a code of football rules that would:

1. be just as common to the whole of Australia as the laws of cricket;
2. provide the requisite recreation to the players; and
3. provide football with greater box office appeal to the public.

Initially, the proposal generated much enthusiasm among the administrators of the two sports. 'Just imagine it,' said James Joynton-Smith, the patron of the NSWRL, 'the game featuring that outstanding high-marking and cultivated drop-kicking of the Australian Rules, and those brilliant passing movements, sizzling wing runs, and the side-stepping and dodging of rugby'.[4]

Shortly after his return to Sydney in late July Miller published a draft set of rules which aimed to do just that.

It envisaged a game of fifteen players per side on an oval pitch. Tries were to be worth three points and goals two points. Rugby league tackle and play-the-ball rules would be used but the scrum would be replaced by the referee bouncing the ball. Offside, in rugby league terminology, would be allowed for players attempting to catch the ball from a punt. Standard rugby posts would be used but the Australian Rules' point posts would be removed. Running with the ball was to be encouraged, and the knock-on and forward pass rules of rugby would be retained, which meant that Rules' bouncing the ball during a run and the hand-pass would be abolished. Full rugby tackling would be allowed, but only from the waist down, and shepherding and tackling airborne players, as allowed in Rules, would be outlawed.[5]

On paper, it seemed to some to be a workable plan.

It was at this point that the cold light of reality began to shine through. Harold 'Jersey' Flegg, chairman of the NSWRL and Miller's great rival, declared that he had no interest in a merged game and would not even attend the conference with the ANFC. 'It involves matters much greater than drafting the new rules ... the original and existing games have their own powerful appeal to their players and public, and [have] the sentiments which history inspires,' he told the press.[6]

The Queensland Rugby League followed Flegg's lead and also refused to participate. Rumours circulated that the idea was merely a publicity stunt to promote the Sydney Carnival, so much so that the ANFC's Mr Stokes felt compelled to deny them.[7]

The question of how the proposals would affect rugby league relations with Britain was also raised. And Con Hickey backtracked somewhat by stating that he was more interested in promoting inter-state contests between NSW and Victoria than a completely new sport. The programme for the Carnival itself contained an article that seemed to discount completely the idea of international competition for the new code; it would be 'a code that would prove popular in every state and be purely national'.[8]

At a practical level, the proposed rules raised more questions than they answered. The most obvious was that Australian Rules did not have an offside rule whereas rugby league had very tightly defined laws on offside. Hickey told the press in a somewhat blasé fashion that the offside problem 'is rather complicated. Still we could look at it from every angle and I have no doubt arrive at a satisfactory conclusion'. Miller's reply was even more unconvincing as he waved aside the potential difficulties with the claim that the NSWRL 'possess a certain amount of administrative and inventive genius'.[9]

The proposal collapsed at the very point at which it should have taken off. On Friday 11 August the first, and only, experimental match was played at Sydney's Agricultural Grounds. It was played fourteen-a-side under slightly different rules to the ones proposed by Miller. Effectively Australian football rules applied in the middle two quarters of the pitch and rugby league rules in each of the end quarters. The two teams were made up of junior Queensland rules players, many of whom allegedly carried sheets of paper with the new rules written on them. Whether this was true or not, the match was clearly a farce and its seriousness for the future of the two sports was demonstrated by the ANFC president, Norwood's E.H. Tassie, who told his companions to expect him back from the match no later than 9pm.[10]

At the NSWRL's general committee meeting the following week, S.G. Ball proposed that the fusion discussions be abandoned and that Miller's report on the discussions should not even be circulated to the NSW clubs. A furious row allegedly broke out between Miller and Jersey Flegg, who accused Miller of disloyalty to the game. Not a single delegate spoke in favour of the fusion and by a margin of fifteen votes to ten it was decided not to circulate the report. The ill-feeling between Miller and Flegg was smoothed over somewhat with the unanimous passing of a motion 'repudiating' suggestions of disloyalty on the part of any members of the committee, although the bad blood between the two continued to flow over the next two decades. Hearing the result of the NSWRL meeting the ANFC council decided to 'take no further action in the matter'.[11]

The fusion proposal died as quickly as it was born and was never raised again.

Uncracking the codes?

But this was not the first time such discussions had been held. Most of the protagonists, not to mention the press, were well aware of two previous meetings that had been held between the two codes to discuss the possibility of fusion, the first in 1908 and the second in 1914.

The first meeting had taken place when the first Australian rugby league touring team departed for Britain from Melbourne in August 1908. Their arrival in Victoria coincided with the Golden Jubilee carnival of Australian Rules, which, like the 1933 Carnival, included Rules teams from every state and also one from New Zealand. Tour managers J.J. Giltinan, Bill Cann and Jack Fihelly met briefly with representatives of the VFL to discuss the possibility of a merged game.[12]

There was undoubtedly a political and possibly entrepreneurial element to this and to the subsequent meetings. The leaders of both the NSWRL and the VFL were skilled in the arts of organisational politics, having decisively defeated their respective incumbent governing bodies, the NSW Rugby Union and the Victorian Football Association (VFA). The arrival of their distant competitors in the cities they dominated would have alerted both their curiosity and their defensive instincts. Attempts, sincere or otherwise, to co-opt a potential threat was an astute tactical move.

The 1908 and 1914 meetings must also be seen in the context of the revolution which was taking place in world rugby in the first decade of the new century. Rugby league's abandonment of the line-out and introduction of the play-the-ball, the reduction in the number of players to thirteen, and the overturning of the amateur shibboleths had put rugby in a state of flux. The idea that those developments could be taken further to incorporate Australian Rules football would not have been perceived as too far-fetched to the men who had led the overthrow of the rugby union authorities in NSW and Queensland.

This self-confidence was clearly apparent in the 1914 meeting. In July of that year a rugby league match had been held in Melbourne between the British touring side and NSW to promote the game in Victoria. The match had been preceded by a Rules game between Beverley and Carlton and on August 4 (a momentous day in history for far more important reasons than mere football) the ANFC voted to organise a conference with the NSWRL to discuss a common set of rules.[13] Although that has generally been thought to be the end of the matter, the two sides actually met on 2 November 1914 and a copy of the minutes of their discussions survives in the J.C. Davis Papers at Sydney's Mitchell Library.

Reading the minutes it is clear that many of the 1933 proposals, and particularly the rules under which the exhibition match was staged, were simply a rehash of these earlier discussions. For example, the idea of the middle half of the pitch being Australian Rules and the two end quarters being rugby league rules comes from this meeting. The pitch itself would measure 170 yards long by 100 yards wide. In the first forty-five yards of each half 'modified rugby league rules' would be played but in the middle seventy yards Australian Rules would be played. Goals were to be eighteen feet wide with a crossbar ten feet high. Tries would be worth three points and goals one point, with a 'flying goal', a goal kicked while running ,would score two points. Teams would be fifteen players per side, the scrum would be replaced with a bounced ball, and the rugby league tackle rule introduced. The aim of these proposals was summed up in the remark of the NSWRL's Ted Mead: 'undoubtedly the foot passing in the Australian game is brilliant, and the hand passing in the Rugby game is brilliant. Would it not be possible to put these features into one game?'

As in 1933, it is also quite clear that neither side had much idea about the other game. The NSWRL's Johnny Quinlan sought to persuade the VFL of the efficacy of scrums: 'The scrum is not dangerous; really very few accidents result. Tackling was regarded as one of the most spectacular features of rugby.' At one point, rugby league's Bill Cann implies that he hasn't even seen a game of Australian Rules: 'he and his co-delegates did not have a grip of the Australian game. He did not think they could get it in a room,' recorded the minutes. The discussion on what rules to retain or discard sounds suspiciously like horse trading: 'if we abolish the scrum, you allow the tackle and abolish hand passing forward', says one of the NSW representatives. The conference lasted two days and ended with the somewhat contradictory recommendation that exhibition matches should be organised but that 'it would be inadvisable at the present juncture to publish the result of their deliberations'. The discussion then fell silent until the start of the 1915 season when the VFL sent a circular to its clubs asking their opinion of the proposed merger rules. League scrums were to be replaced by a bounce-up and VFL posts would have a crossbar added. The VFL would allow tackling between the hip and the shoulder. League passing would be allowed but knock-forwards would be classed as knock-ons. By 7-2, the VFL clubs agreed to the changes, with only Carlton and Richmond dissenting. But the outbreak of World War One had thrown the VFL into turmoil over whether to continue playing during the war and the merger question was forgotten as Australia flung itself into battle against the Kaiser.[14]

But by 1933 the world had moved on. Rugby league had

consolidated and deepened its position as the dominant football code in NSW and Queensland while Australian rules stood unchallenged as the football code of the southern states. Given the obvious problems with the idea of a fusion, one must ask why it was mooted again. The fact that it was only being raised at the time of the Sydney carnival - and the proposal had only ever been raised when either a big rugby league match was held in Melbourne or a major Australian rules event was held in Sydney - suggests that there was an element of public relations and political manoeuvring to it.

Economic factors also perhaps played a role. In 1914 the NSWRL was dissatisfied with the poor returns it was making on both outgoing and incoming tours; the 1908 tour to England had made a huge loss, for example. The depression of the early 1930s had reduced spectator numbers at club matches in Sydney to some extent, but for finals and internationals crowds remained robustly healthy. The first Test match of the 1932 Ashes series brought 70,204 people to the Sydney Cricket Ground, then the biggest crowd ever at a football match in Australia and one which would not be exceeded at a VFL Grand Final until 1938. The prospect of a game that could offer regular inter-state matches would have been attractive to the NSWRL, especially if the matches could replicate the success of cricket clashes between NSW and Victoria. But, perhaps more importantly, the 1933 discussions must also be seen in the context of the bitter rivalry between Horrie Miller and Jersey Flegg in the leadership of the NSWRL. Despite (or perhaps because of) being related by marriage, there was a deep personal animosity between the two. There can be no doubt that Miller saw his gambit with Australian Rules as an opportunity to establish an unquestioned authority over Flegg and the NSWRL as a whole. Its failure left Miller isolated in the NSWRL hierarchy and Flegg was eventually to deliver his coup de grace in 1946 when Miller was cruelly ousted in a minor financial scandal.

For Australian Rules, even the slightest opportunity to become the all-Australia code of football made the discussions worthwhile, although the fact that the 1933 Sydney Carnival made a loss of £1,000 and attracted barely 49,000 spectators over seven days may have helped cool the ANFC's enthusiasm. But it is clear from the transcripts of the 1914 discussions and from the ANFC minutes for 1933 that there was a degree of genuine interest in exploring the possibilities on the part of at least some of the participants. The VFL may also have seen the talks as a way of gaining at least a public relations advantage over their rivals in the VFA, which was not a member of the ANFC. It may be argued that the fact that the discussions were conducted through the ANFC and not the VFL, the real power in Australian Rules, demonstrated a lack of seriousness about the proposals. However, although the ANFC had occasionally disagreed with the VFL, in general it followed the lead of the VFL. The fact that Fitzroy's Con Hickey, the VFL's organising secretary since 1910, initiated and led the discussions demonstrates the VFL's leadership in the matter. And the VFL itself voted unanimously to support the initiative.[15]

Despite this, none of the discussions appear to have sparked even the curiosity of football supporters in Melbourne or Sydney. Indeed, it is difficult to find any report of the proposals or discussions in the Melbourne press. The 1933 discussion ended almost as soon as the Sydney carnival was over without a single public voice being raised in favour of the proposal, lending weight to the idea that 'merger' was merely a public relations exercise. As senior VFL official Charles Brownlow noted during the 1914 discussions, 'the supreme test must necessarily be public approval'. But the sporting public of NSW and Victoria did not show any interest in, much less approved of, an artificial attempt by administrators to suck a new sport out of their thumbs.

Rugby's tree of evolution

Despite obviously having no chance of success in meeting their aim of fusion, the discussions are important for historians because of the light they shed on evolution of the non-soccer codes of football. On the evolutionary tree of football, Australian Rules emerged from the same branch as the other handling codes, albeit slightly earlier. Although it is often claimed that the Australian game is unique, this is geographic rather than a technical judgement. Indeed, there is a much stronger argument that soccer, despite its ubiquity, is the unique code of football because of its prohibition on handling the ball and tightly prescribed tackling laws. As Gillian Hibbins, among others, has pointed out in her seminal article on the origins of Australian Rules, the origins of the sport can be traced directly back to the football played at Rugby school.[16] The use of the rugby-derived ball, the mark and even behinds - variants of which were used in rugby in the 1880s - demonstrate the survival of rugby DNA in the bloodstream of Australian Rules even today.

As late as the 1940s it was common for English visitors to Australia to refer to the sport as 'Australian rugby', including Eddie Waring who watched games in Perth and Melbourne while travelling with the 1946 British league touring side.[17] Although regional and cultural differences have played significant roles in the evolution of the handling codes, much of the development of the laws of the games of league, Australian, American, Canadian and, more recently, rugby union football was and is based on developing solutions to the problems posed by the original rules of Rugby football. The two key problems with which the codes have always grappled are those of the importance of offside and what to do when a player is tackled in possession of the ball.

The offside issue was one of the first to be settled in Australian Rules through the simple expedient of not having an offside rule. For the other codes, their more direct links with rugby rules meant that offside was more problematic. The American and Canadian games overcame the shortcomings of the complexities of rugby's offside by sanctioning the forward pass and allowing receivers to run downfield. From a present-day perspective, league has not moved as far from its rugby roots, but in 1933 there was significant tension between the offside rule and the way the game was played. It was this which meant that for some league followers the fusion discussions were not totally absurd.

Looking at footage of the 1932 rugby league Ashes Test series in Australia, one can see that a major feature of the game was the kicking duel, in which each side's full-back would kick the ball far down field, hoping to catch the opposite full-back out of position or force a mistake. The British captain on that tour, full-back Jim Sullivan, was a master of this tactic. But the offside rule meant that players could not advance on the opposing full-back unless he moved, and two good full-backs could keep a kicking duel going for many minutes, effectively bringing the game to a halt. The idea that the offside rule should be suspended so that the full-back could be challenged when catching the ball may have had some appeal, especially if it led to the introduction of the flying mark. The rule discussions could therefore have been seen as a way of revivifying the mark in rugby league, which had practically died out (although it did not finally disappear from the rule book until the 1960s) and had become a stultifying defensive tactic in union, thus potentially opening up the game even more. It is interesting that in 1914 Charles Brownlow noted that John Clifford, the manager of the English league touring side, had commented how much he liked features of the Australian game, such as the long kicking and each player taking his own shot at goal, both of which had been features of rugby when Clifford had played in the 1880s.[18]

For the Australian Rules side, the discussions were a way of engaging with the second and most intractable problem that bedevils all handling forms of football: what to do with the ball when the player with the ball is tackled? American and Canadian football had solved the question with the development of the snap at the line of scrimmage and rugby league had done so by allowing the tackled player to rise with the ball and play it to a team-mate standing behind. But in this respect Australian Rules, although more fluid than its cousin codes, had remained somewhat closer to its rugby union roots than these other games. Its insistence that once a player was held by a tackler the ball had to be disposed of, by either dropping, kicking or hand-passing it, was closely related to the rugby union principle that a tackled player on the ground had to release the ball to allow it to be played by the feet. However, the reality of playing football meant that players were unwilling to release the ball when it was not to their advantage. Furthermore, the uncertain mechanics of retrieving the released ball meant that ugly loose scrummaging in rugby union or scrambling for the ball on the ground in Australian Rules would quite often be the result.

As much was conceded by Charles Brownlow in the 1914 discussions: 'one very fine point was when a man was caught or when he was only touched, it was not a satisfactory point in the Australian game, and the players here might be able to adopt the rugby tackle in a modified form'. Con Hickey was also critical of his sport's tackling rules in the 1933 discussions and told the *Referee* that the league rule would 'wipe out a tremendous lot of the free kicks now given in our game'.[19] In the years following World War One the question of the 'holding man-ball rule' had been debated several times by the VFL and the rule had been amended in 1928, 1930 and 1939. Indeed the 1930 change to the rule - whereby the held player could not simply drop the ball but had to kick or handpass it - had proved so controversial that it had been withdrawn by the VFL after just two months.[20]

It may well have been the case at the time that, from a Australian Rules perspective, the rugby league play-the-ball rule - an evolutionary mid-point between the uncontrolled rugby union release of the ball and the totally controlled North American snap - would have appeared to be one solution to the scramble on the ground following the surrender of the ball during a tackle.

Perhaps paradoxically, the discussions on how to merge the rules of the two games underlined the extent to which Australian Rules was historically a form of rugby. Leaving aside the practicalities of changing the culture of the two sports, the fundamental problem of the merged rules that were drawn up in 1914 and 1933 was that they would lead to the league-derived rules being quickly abandoned. For if there was no offside rule, why should players bother passing the ball or even scoring tries?

The most effective tactic would be to kick the ball as far as possible downfield with the aim of scoring goals. Hickey himself anticipated that this would be a problem during the 1914 discussion, arguing the rules players would not 'attack in the sense understood by the Rugby players. They would be more likely to shoot the ball from one point to another, and secure a goal before an attack could be developed.' Indeed, league dealt was to deal with a similar problem in the early 1970s when, with tries then worth three points and drop-goals two points, a number of teams used the tactic of simply advancing downfield with the aim of scoring a drop-goal rather than expending extra effort in attempting to score tries. The solution was to reduce the value of a drop-goal to one point in 1974. But the offside rule was the glue that held the passing game together. Without it, the game would become primarily a kicking game, demonstrating that Australian Rules was, in effect, rugby without offside.

Politics on and off the pitch

One of the most intriguing and speculative points about the 1933 merger discussion is its broader political context. The discussion took place just six months after the end of the Bodyline cricket tour. The future of the 1934 Australian cricket tour to England was still in doubt and popular hostility to at least certain aspects of Britain had never been higher. Given the Labourite, left-wing outlook of a number of the officials of the NSWRL (especially Miller, who was rumoured to be sympathetic to the Communist Party in the early 1940s), it is interesting to ask whether the impulse to create an 'All-Australia' game was connected to a desire to break the link with Britain.

Certainly the question of relations with British sport was central to much of the press coverage of the merger proposals. The headlines in the *Referee* the week after the discussions were announced read 'Can England be brought into new football? International element is vital. What will happen if England versus Australia is lost by fusion?'[21]

Much discussion from the Sydney side centred on how the link could be maintained, including the possibility that the English Rugby Football League would adopt the new game. There was even a suggestion that even if a new game were adopted in Australia internationals could still be played under league rules. However, there was absolutely no discussion or even mention of the merger question in England - in fact, there is no evidence to suggest that it was even known about, despite the Australian touring team being on its way to Britain. Much of Jersey Flegg's opposition to the plan was based on the fact that rugby league's traditions were firmly British. He told a reporter that 'he takes pride in the British tone and atmosphere of rugby and ... will not have the fusion at any price.'[22] And an editorial in the *Sydney Morning Herald* stressed the common argument of league and union opponents of Australian Rules: 'rugby has something to offer its outstanding exponents which no manufactured article can ever do - something visible at this moment in the spectacle of the Wallabies playing in South Africa and the Kangaroos drawing near to England.'[23]

It was also noted by Davis and others that the sport which had the strongest claim to be Australia's national football code was rugby union, given that it was played elite private schools in all of Australia's major cities and had the widest international links. There was an element of truth in this. Rugby union had made small but not insignificant progress among the Melbourne professional classes in the 1930s and in 1932 Edward 'Weary' Dunlop had become the first Victorian-born rugby union player to be selected for Australia. In 1939 four Victorian players who were picked to go on the ill-fated Wallaby tour of Britain.[24] Davis also suggested, perhaps seeking to justify his pen-name of 'Cynic' that the easiest way to get a national football code would be for everyone to adopt 'one of the British football games, rugby union, league or soccer. But that, of course, would not suit the men of the South.'[25]

The lack of an international dimension undermined Australian Rules' credibility as a truly representative national sport and had been something of a raw nerve for the leaders of Australian Rules football. In his autobiography, H.C.A. Harrison recorded his disappointment in not being able to establish the game in London during his trip there in 1884. The visit of the unofficial and unashamedly commercial British rugby union team in 1888, which played nineteen games of Australian Rules in its fifty-three match tour, falsely raised hopes that they would establish the game in Britain on their return. At its August 1911 meeting the ANFC spent a long time discussing the potential for overseas expansion and whether to support J.J. Simons' evangelical tour to the USA. The NSW delegates supported Simons by pointing out that 'Rugby men' tempted young players with the argument that 'there was a chance of a trip to England with them, while under Australian Rules there was no possibility of an international trip'.[26] The withering and demise of the sport's roots in New Zealand before the First World War had removed its only non-Australian outpost, locking it into Australia alone.

But the sport's lack of an overt British link was also an attractive feature to those Australians who had a more consciously nationalist political outlook. And although the vast majority of Australian Rules administrators were loyal to the Empire - as the sport's support for World War One and the singing of *God Save the King* at Grand Finals demonstrated - there appears to have been a tension between its Britishness and Australianness which was not apparent in the other football codes. To take two examples that were probably unthinkable elsewhere, in 1906 the

ANFC adopted the slogan, echoing that of Federation, of 'One Flag, One Destiny, One Football Game: the Australian'. And, in a more extreme case, Simons' nationalist and deeply racist Young Australian League, based in Western Australia, vigorously promoted Australian Rules football as a supposedly native alternative to 'British' soccer.[27] This tension also came to the fore in the 1933 discussions. In response to qualms in Sydney about breaking the link with Britain, an ANFC committee member told the press bluntly, 'we should search for a game for Australia and forget about England for the present'.[28]

To what extent did Australian Rules appear to the sporting public to be a nationalist alternative to 'British' codes of football during the inter-war period? In 1931 *The Australian Game of Football* claimed that

> there is something analogous in the rapid growth of the Australian nation to the extraordinary progress made by the Australian game of football. It has been said that there is no form of sport more expressive of the characteristics which have come to be associated with our people than this game, which is purely of local development.[29]

But the assertion that a type of football was a unique reflection of local characteristics was also a common one within England itself: rugby league and Lancashire and Yorkshire, soccer and the North East, rugby union and Cornwall to name just three examples.

Regardless of the truth of these often romanticised claims, the identification of difference, as expressed through sport, was not necessarily an expression of hostility to, or a desire to separate from, Imperial Britain.

In general, the question of the link between political nationalism and sport is a difficult one to answer. The simple binary opposition of the sporting contest cannot simply be used as a guide to political feeling. Nor should we fall into the trap of viewing sporting organisations as analogous to political parties. Contemporary popular perceptions of sports are also difficult for historians to discern, due to the necessary reliance on official minutes and newspaper reports. And perceptions of sports can also be extremely contradictory.

For example, rugby league historically saw itself as both as an egalitarian working-class game and a loyally British sport. It is probable that Australian Rules also saw itself in a similarly contradictory way, as a distinctly Australian variation of the British game of 'football'. The fact that it was a code of football that was not played in Britain did not necessarily make it non-British. It was only in the 1920s that football became a synonym for soccer in the UK, rather than a generic name for all codes of the sport.

The current perception that Rules football is part of a unique and distinct Australian way of life that is *counterposed* to Britain and 'Britishness' can probably be traced back to the breaking of the imperial link and the growth of 'social nationalism' in the 1960s. But for at least the period up to the 1960s it is perhaps safe to assume that for some of the minority of Australians who did want to break the British link, Australian Rules was the sport with which they could be most comfortable. The fact that this was an issue that was present but never really addressed in the 1933 merger discussions is indicative of the complexities of the issues surrounding sport and Australian nationalism in the inter-war years.[30]

Conclusion

To a large extent the 1933 episode is deservedly a footnote in football history, a counter-factual curiosity to enliven the dull fare of the football encyclopedia.

However, its apparent oddness means that there are also important points for the historiography of sport that can be drawn out. The evolution of the football codes as a whole and the similarities between them have too often been overlooked or downplayed. In fact, as the 1933 merger discussions revealed, all the handling codes of football, and even soccer to a much more limited extent, have had to deal with similar technical problems in the development of their systems and rules of playing the game. And, as the unanimous apathy toward the 1933 proposals suggests, the cultural and emotional hold of a sport over its supporters is not just confined to a shared sense of time, place and tradition. It is also embedded in a sport's rules, which offer a distinctiveness that underpins the identity of supporters with not only their clubs but also with the sport itself.

On a broader level, this type of unusual event is also useful for the historian because it can throw into relief issues such as national, gender and class identity. An underlying aspect of the merger proposals was the debate on the importance of Britain to Australia. The deep reluctance of the Sydney side of the discussion to break or challenge the British sporting link, coming so soon after the crisis of the Bodyline, challenges the traditional narrative that the actions of Douglas Jardine's English cricketers caused a wholesale reconsideration of, and challenge to, the imperial link with Britain. The episode also highlights the complexities of nationalism in the context of sport; sporting opposition on the field of play or difference in the code of rules does not necessarily translate into political or national separatism.

Perhaps Horrie Miller and Con Hickey did believe that the 'Universal Football League' would be greater than the sum of its parts. However, as the marketing consultants and business planners behind the Super League 'vision' of the mid-1990s and club mergers in the different football codes over the past twenty years have discovered, abstract logic and so-called business sense have little to do with supporters' affiliation to his or her football code or club. Whatever logic was behind the 1933 merger discussions, it appealed to no-one but a handful of administrators. Perhaps the final word on the matter should be left to an anonymous leader writer in the *Sydney Morning Herald*. 'Each game is too well-rooted in its own sphere to be shaken and any attempt thereat would almost surely bring nothing but *disappointment* and *disaster*.'[31] This is a lesson that football administrators, of whatever code, and media moguls should heed.

Notes

[1] This chapter is based on 'One Common Code of Football for Australia!: The Australian Rules and Rugby League Merger Proposal of 1933' in Rob Hess, Matthew Nicholson and Bob Stewart (eds) *Football Fever: Crossing Boundaries,* Melbourne: Maribyrnong Press, 2005. Much of the research for this article was made possible by the award of a fellowship by the Council for Australian State Libraries in 2004-05. I would also like to thank Mark Hildebrand and Andy Carr at the State Library of New South Wales for their help and support, and Mary Bushby, Braham Dabscheck and Don Selth for their comments on an early draft of the paper. The name 'Universal Football League' for the new venture is in the *Sydney Morning Herald*, 12 August, 1933.

[2] *Referee*, 7 July 1933.

[3] This and the following quote is from the *Referee*, 13 July 1933.

[4] *Referee*, 7 July 1933.

[5] *Referee*, 27 July 1933.

1895 & All That...

[6] *Referee*, 8 August 1933

[7] Australian National Football Council minutes, 8 August 1933.

[8] *Australian National Football Carnival Record 1933 Official Programme*, p. 4.

[9] *Referee*, 7 July 1933.

[10] *Referee*, 17 August 1933. *The Age*, 14 August 1933.

[11] *Rugby League News* (Sydney), 19 August 1933. Australian National Football Council, addendum to the minutes of 8 August 1933. The dispute between Miller and Flegg is recounted by journalist Tom Goodman in Ian Heads, *True Blue: The Story of the NSWRL*, Sydney 1992, p. 202.

[12] *Rugby League News* [Sydney], 15 July 1933. See also Gary Lester, *The Story of Australian Rugby League*, Sydney 1988, p. 48.

[13] *Daily Telegraph* [Sydney], 12 August 1914. *Referee* 19 August 1914.

[14] All quotations from the preceding two paragraphs are from *Report of Conference between the Australian Football League [sic] and the New South Wales Rugby League*, 2 and 6 November 1914: Mitchell Library, J.C. Davis Collection, Box 21. *Football Record*, 23 April 1915, p. 7.

[15] *Referee*, 14 July, 1933.

[16] G. M. Hibbins, 'The Cambridge Connection: The English Origins of Australian Rules Football' in J. A. Mangan (ed.) *The Cultural Bond. Sport, Empire, Society*. London, 1993. See also Robin Grow, 'From Gum Trees to Goalposts, 1858-1876' in Rob Hess and Bob Stewart (eds) *More than a Game*, Melbourne, 1998 and Geoffrey Blainey, *A Game of Our Own*, Melbourne, revised edition, 2003.

[17] Eddie Waring, *England to Australia and New Zealand*, Leeds 1947, p. 17. Newsreels of VFL Grand Finals shown in British cinemas in the 1940s also referred to the sport as Australian rugby.

[18] Australasian Football Council, minutes, 4 August 1914.

[19] *Referee*, 7 July 1933.

[20] The debate about releasing the ball continues today. See, for example, a discussion about players deliberately not releasing the ball when held on *The Footy Show* (AFL edition), 16 June, 2004.

[21] *Referee*, 27 July 1933.

[22] *Referee*, 3 August 1933.

[23] *Sydney Morning Herald*, 4 August 1933.

[24] *Referee*, 7 July 1933. *Rugby News*, 14 August 1933.

[25] *Referee*, 3 August 1933.

[26] H.C.A. Harrison, *The Story of an Athlete*, Melbourne, 1923, p. 99. Australasian Football Council minutes, 5 August 1911.

[27] See Simons' magazine *Australia Junior*, vol. 2 (undated, c. 1907), in the J.C. Davis Collection.

[28] *Sydney Morning Herald*, 3 August 1933.

[29] J.F. McHale, A.E. Chadwick and E.C.H. Taylor, *The Australian Game of Football*, Melbourne, 1931, p. 1.

[30] For an extended discussion on the links between sport and nationalism in Australia see, among many others, W.F. Mandle, 'Cricket and Australian Nationalism in the Nineteenth Century', *Journal of the Royal Australian Historical Society*, 59, December, 1973 and Richard Cashman, *Sport in the National Imagination*, Petersham, 2002.

[31] *Sydney Morning Herald*, 4 August 1933. Emphasis in original.

The 1932 Lions - as seen in Australia

13

Arrogant Aussies & Whinging Poms:
An Alternative History of the
Rugby League Ashes

Test matches between Australia and Great Britain traditionally have been magnificent in their drama but brutal in their intensity.

'To call it a game is a misnomer,' wrote the *Yorkshire Post* about the famous 0-0 third Ashes Test match of 1930. 'War is a more appropriate term.' The second Test match of the 1932 Ashes series, the Battle of Brisbane, was described as 'hard all the time, rough most of the time and foul frequently'.[1]

Bradford's Ken Traill called the third Test of 1952, the Battle of Bradford, the roughest game he had ever experienced. The 1970 World Cup final at Headingley became infamous for its vicious fighting, which did not end when the referee sounded the final whistle. These were just two of the most notorious examples.[2]

The violence of Ashes Test matches is often seen as an example of how sport played a vital in creating Australian national identity. Sporting contests between Britain and Australia, whether at rugby league, cricket or rugby union, seem to reflect the national and political hostility of Australia to Britain and the British Empire. The Barrow-born historian of Australia, W.F. Mandle, has argued that from the late 1800s sport has been a barometer of Australian nationalist or separatist feeling.[3] The most famous example is cricket's 1932-33 'Bodyline' tour, when the intimidating bowling tactics of England captain Douglas Jardine led to a diplomatic dispute between the British and Australian governments.

But the reality is not quite so straight forward. It was the Australians who backed down over Bodyline and apologised to the British. And for all of the mutual hostility between the Lions and the Kangaroos on the pitch, off it more united them than divided them. In fact, the history of rugby league contests between the two offer a fascinating window on the story of Anglo-Australian relations in the twentieth century.

An Anglo-Australian sport

The origins of rugby league in Australia can be traced back to 1907 when a team of New Zealand rugby players broke from the domestic rugby union authorities and toured Britain to play the new rugby game. On their way to Britain they played in Sydney and helped to provide one of the catalysts that led to the formation of the New South Wales Rugby League (NSWRL) and a similar body in Queensland.[4]

The new sport spread rapidly through the rugby strongholds of NSW and Queensland, not least because it was closely associated with the working class and its culture. As in Britain, there had been simmering discontent among rugby union's growing base of working-class players and supporters throughout the early years of the century, highlighted by disputes over the lack of compensation paid to injured working-class players, most famously in the case of Alec Burdon of Glebe. Tightly controlled by members of the professional and managerial middle-classes, the Australian rugby union authorities took their lead from the English RFU and attempted to impose strict amateurism on rugby, not least as a means of keeping in check the burgeoning working-class involvement in the game.

Although rugby league was promoted by sporting entrepreneurs such as the Australian cricketer Victor Trumper and the businessman Sir James Joynton-Smith, the sport was from the outset, as Andrew Moore has pointed out, 'strongly circumscribed within a labour universe, a reflection of the self-confidence and sense of separate identity of a working-class movement recovering from the defeats of the 1890s. Drawing upon a value system that prized masculinity, aggression and local identity, the game tapped into aspects of working-class life.'[5]

Harry Hoyle, the first president of the NSWRL, was a prominent activist in the railway workers' union and an Australian Labor Party election candidate. Ted Larkin, the league's first full-time secretary, was elected as an ALP member of the NSW parliament in 1913. Many of the founding clubs of the NSWRL had prominent ALP or trade union leaders as committee members or patrons. Future prime minister Billy Hughes was the patron of Glebe, while North Sydney's patron was Teddy Clark, the first president of the cabman's union. John Storey, who became NSW premier in 1920, was a founder of the Balmain club. In Queensland, the central figure in the split from rugby union was Jack Fihelly, the future deputy leader of the Queensland ALP and prominent Irish nationalist.

Fihelly also symbolised the strong link between the sport and Catholicism in Queensland. Similar ties were established in early in the game's history in NSW. Ted

Larkin sought to establish the game in Catholic schools before World War One and in 1918 Christian Brothers' schools affiliated to the NSWRL, followed by Marist Brothers' in 1926.[6] By the 1930s these links with the labour movement had been deepened and extended, to the extent that between 1934 and 1950 the trophy for the winners of the Sydney club competition was provided by the *Labor Daily*, the newspaper founded by the Miners' Federation and run by supporters of NSW Labor Party prime minister Jack Lang in the 1930s.

Tours to and from Australia were a central feature of rugby league culture. The first Australian tour to Britain took place in 1908, the first British tour to Australia two years later, and, interrupted only by world wars, they continued on a four-year cycle until the mid-1990s. Based on the format of cricket tours, the centrepiece of each tour was a series of three Test matches, the overall victor of which would win the rugby league 'Ashes'. Lacking the links to the imperial elite of cricket or rugby union but, unlike Australian Rules football, able to compete regularly at an international level with British representatives, rugby league seemed to provide an arena in which national antagonisms could be played out at their most intense. Indeed, the fierce rivalry between the Australian and British national teams appeared to be a graphic illustration of Australian self-assertion and hostility to British rule.

The first Test match between the two countries to be held in Australia in 1910 set the tone. It was, said the *Referee*, a 'rough, foul game'. The resumption of matches after the First World War revealed that little had changed. 'The contest was not characterised by anything striking in sportsmanship: that is, the striking things done were with fists or boots,' wrote one reporter about the first Test match of the 1920 series.

The tone intensified even more in the 1930s. After the second Test of the 1932 tour, the 'Battle of Brisbane', Claude Corbett, probably Australia's leading league journalist of the time, called for a clamp-down on violent play 'otherwise there will be a fatality on the field which will not be accidental'. In 1936 Australian forward Ray Stehr achieved the still unique feat of being sent off twice in the same Ashes series.

It appears that officials were often as culpable as the players. The British winger Alf Ellaby blamed the tour managers for 'indoctrinating' players in the dressing room before Test matches and remembered as 'disgusting' the speech given before the first Test match of 1928 in Brisbane. Some support for this view was provided by Claude Corbett, who claimed in 1932 that British players had told him that 'they acted in a way which would not have permitted them to stay five minutes in the game at home'.[7]

Post-war British RFL secretary Bill Fallowfield certainly had little truck with those who criticised the exuberance of touring teams: 'rugby league players are not supposed to be cissies,' he told journalists in 1952 in response to criticisms that the Australian tourists were overly physical in their approach to the game. In 1958 Ray Stehr, now a prominent journalist, noted that it wasn't only the players who felt it necessary to resolve their differences through fisticuffs when he recalled, perhaps exaggeratedly, a fight in the team hotel between Australian tour manager Wally Webb and Bradford chairman Harry Hornby in 1934.[8]

Looking at this evidence, it would be easy to conclude that rugby league reflected a deep Australian hostility to Britain and its Empire. What's more, given its ties to the labour movement, widespread support in Catholic communities and the overwhelmingly working-class composition of its teams and crowds, Australian rugby league was in many ways representative of what historian Gavin Souter described as 'those who in varying degrees had rejected, outgrown, forgotten or simply never known the British inheritance. To [this] group, which might be called the indigenous Australians, belonged a large part of the working class, most Irish Catholics, the children of European immigrants, the industrially militant and the politically radical.'[9] Souter argues that these Australians were the wellspring of nationalist feeling. Rugby league therefore seems to be the perfect example of Australian sporting nationalism.

However, this is not the case. In fact, the representatives of Australian rugby league were unashamed in their Britishness and vocal in their support for the Empire.

This can be seen throughout the early years of the sport in Australia. Welcoming the first British touring team to Australia in 1910 James Joynton-Smith, president of the NSWRL, assured the visitors that they 'could rely absolutely on getting British fair play,' following which his guests were treated to a rendition of 'God Save the King'. Up to and including the 1921-22 visit to Britain, the touring side included New Zealanders and was known as the Australasian team, representing a region of the Empire rather than national aspirations.

In 1926 the NSWRL (historically the most important body in the Australian game) invited Britain to send a touring team over a year ahead of the normal cycle of four-yearly tours, because they felt that 1927 would be 'an appropriate occasion for the visit of an English team, in view of the Duke of York's visit to Canberra'. At a dinner in honour of the 1928 British tourists, Harry Sunderland, a leading Queensland rugby league official, told the visitors to 'remember Captain Cook; if he hadn't planted the Union Jack here, Australia might have become a Dutch dependency'.

In 1928 Sydney's City Tattersall's club presented a trophy

to be awarded to the winner of the Ashes Test series, expressing the hope that they were 'helping to perpetuate the true sporting spirit which is characteristic of all sporting bodies in the British Empire.' Perhaps most the most notable of these expressions of loyalty came from Australian foreign minister and future Labour Party leader H.V. Evatt, who in October 1945 addressed an RFL council meeting in Manchester to persuade it to organise a tour of Australia. 'The close relationships that have been built up between Australia and New Zealand and the North of England is in the nature of a history and the building up of this history ought to be resumed as soon as possible, in the best interests of rugby league football and of the Empire,' he told the meeting.[10]

These sentiments continued to be expressed well into the 1950s. 'We are just as British as you are,' protested Harry 'Jersey' Flegg, the president of the New South Wales Rugby League, in 1950 during an argument with British tour manager George Oldroyd. This view was reiterated strenuously four years later by E.S. Brown, who addressed the British RFL Council on behalf of the Australian governing body: 'Australians look to England as the mother country in war, in industry and also in rugby league football'.

He went on to explain that 'there is a strong desire to in Australia to get along with England from every point of view'. This view was more than backed up by the Australian sporting press until the 1960s. The 1914 third Test in Sydney was named 'the Rorke's Drift Test' - in favourable comparison to the 1879 rearguard action fought by a hundred British troops in South Africa against King Cetshwayo's Zulu armies in January 1879 - not by British but by Australian journalists. Even as late as 1958 the Australian *Truth* could begin its report of the second Test match, again a landmark British victory against overwhelming odds, by quoting Shakespeare: 'This happy breed of men, this little world ... this England.'[11]

How Australian was Australian sport?

This apparent contradiction between imperial loyalty and ferocious sporting rivalry can be explained if we compare Australian sporting culture not with that of the south of England, but of the industrial north.

There has long been an unquestioned assumption among historians that Australian sporting values and attitudes were distinctive and, in the main, counterposed to those of England. W.F. Mandle identifies forthrightness, egalitarianism and opposition to snobbishness as the key distinguishing features of Australian sporting culture.[12] But, leaving aside the contentious implication that Australian sport was free of social discrimination, these characteristics were far from unique. They could just as easily be ascribed to sport in northern England.

The counties of Lancashire and Yorkshire were associated with frankness and 'speaking one's mind' almost to the extent of parody. Criticism of snobbishness in British sport was common in the north, especially in those sports which had a mass working-class following, such as cricket, soccer and rugby league. Explicit and implicit criticism of the hypocrisy of amateurism, of favouritism shown towards members of the southern English middle classes and of the division of sport into the 'classes and the masses' was a feature of the writings of northern sports journalists and newspapers such as the *Athletic News* from the 1880s onwards. For example, widespread admiration of the prodigious talents of W.G. Grace did not stop northern commentators from attacking his 'shamateurism' or the favours shown to him by the English cricket authorities.

Closely connected to this hostility to aristocratic and upper middle-class control of British sport was a strong sense of regional sporting identity that defined itself very much in opposition to the metropolitan centre. This was particularly noticeable in cricket matches between the leading northern county cricket clubs, Lancashire, Nottinghamshire and Yorkshire, and Middlesex and Surrey, the exemplars of southern privilege in the eyes of many northerners.[13] But this antagonism was even more apparent within rugby before and after the 1895 split when the strict amateurism of the southern-based RFU was identified by many in the North as an excuse for hypocrisy and snobbery.

One of the most acute expressions was to be found in the late 1880s and early 1890s when the reward for the winners of rugby's county championship was a match against the England team. Northern counties won the championship every year before the 1895 split and the game against England became the occasion for expressions of antagonism towards southern England. If one substitutes 'England' for the South and 'Australia' for the North, the sentiments of this representative passage from the *Yorkshireman* magazine in 1890 echo those found in the pages of the Australian nationalist journal *Bulletin* in the 1890s or in the popular press at the height of the Bodyline controversy:

> For years the South has been the 'be all and end all' of English football. But this privilege is a thing of the past. The centre of English football has been transferred to the North, and to Yorkshire particularly. It Southerners don't recognise this cordially they will have to be made to do so.[14]

This hostility to 'the South' as the embodiment of middle-class traditional Englishness was deeply rooted in the worldview of rugby league and its followers. But it did not see itself as anti-British or separatist. Its conception of Britain was industrial, meritocratic and egalitarian - indeed, it was very similar to how many Australians saw, or would like to see, their own society.

This was not the only way in which sport in northern England resembled that in Australia. 'Barracking', the Australian term for spectators shouting with varying degrees of hostility at players or match officials, has been held up by Mandle and many others as a distinctive feature of the Australian way of sport.[15] Yet this was a common feature of soccer, cricket and rugby crowds in the north from at least the 1880s.

The experiences of Australian rugby league tourists to Britain suggests a strong case for arguing that the phenomenon was actually more pronounced in the north than it was in Australia. For example, Chris McKivat, the captain of the Australasian rugby league side that toured Britain in 1911-12, complained at a farewell dinner at the end of the tour that, 'on some grounds the conduct of your spectators is much worse than we have in Australia. You take your defeats far too seriously.' In 1948 full-back Clive Churchill played in the Australian tourists' first match of their British tour at Huddersfield and discovered that 'the English crowds were viciously patriotic towards their own players. English crowds, in fact, are one-eyed and shockingly partisan.'[16]

Highly competitive, partisan, hostile to privilege and egalitarian; these were features of northern English sport as much as they were Australian. And this was especially true of rugby league, in many ways the quintessentially northern sport.

A poem published in the Manchester-based *Athletic News*

in 1910 on the eve of the departure of the first British rugby league tour to Australia expressed the values of sport in the North in a way with which most Australians could easily identify:

> You're not of the bluest blood, boys,
> Not aristocrats, what then?
> You're something that's quite as good, boys,
> You're honest young Englishmen.
> And what does it matter the rank, boys,
> 'Tis better that you should claim
> That you are straightforward and frank, boys,
> And keen upon 'Playing the Game'.[17]

The themes of the poem reflect British rugby league's view of itself: honest, straightforward, frank and critical of privilege ('what does it matter the rank'). These were qualities central to self-image of the North of England - and were also the values that were promoted by Australians as being specific to Australian sport. And, as the poem implies, class was central to the construction and articulation of this discourse. Just as in the North of England, much of the Australian criticism of 'English' sport was actually a critique of English upper- and middle-class mores and values.

The condemnation of Douglas Jardine during the Bodyline tour (and, to a lesser extent, the violence of touring British rugby union sides) was in large part based on the perceived hypocrisy of what he represented: a member of an upper class that spoke about 'fair play' in life and in sport yet did not practise it. This was exactly the complaint of northern English sports followers about the southern-based sporting authorities. It should also be noted that class snobbery was also central to much of the hostility of the British upper- and middle-classes towards Australia. This was perhaps best exemplified by the belief of English upper-class novelist Angela Thirkell that Australia was 'an entire continent peopled by the Lower Orders'.[18]

British rugby league teams that toured Australia therefore stood in marked contrast to the dominant perceptions of Britishness, both in Britain and Australia. Captained and led by workers from the industrial heartlands of Britain - almost certainly a unique phenomenon among imperial travellers in the first half of the century - the British players were working men just as the Australian players and spectators were. They thus presented an image of the Empire which appeared to resemble Australia more than it did Britain; ostensibly meritocratic and egalitarian, yet still very much British.

'The most democratic of sports...'

The consciousness of class was deeply woven into the fabric of the culture of rugby league in both countries. However, this was not a class consciousness that saw the working class having interests fundamentally opposed to capitalism or to other classes. At its most 'political' it reflected a belief that the division within rugby demonstrated how society was divided into 'us and them'. Rather than class conflict, its goal was the equality of the working class in the life of the nation. Writing in 1941 the secretary of the NSWRL, Horrie Miller, explicitly laid out this philosophy when he wrote that rugby league:

> is a game for every class and all classes to play. It is not a caste game. Any game which brings together, on the field of sport, men and boys of every type, must be a nation-builder ... it is essential that every class in a community should understand and appreciate the worth of every other class.[19]

The idea that the rugby league had a quasi-political purpose was also reflected by the way in which it described itself in both Britain and Australia.

As early as 1914, the manager of that year's British touring team, John Houghton, had defined the purpose of the tourists: 'their mission was to propagate their game of [rugby league] football because they believed it was the people's game'. From the 1920s onward it became commonplace in Australia for the sport to refer to itself as the 'people's code'. It also sought to promote itself explicitly as a democratic game. Eddie Waring, the famous English sports journalist, claimed on many occasions that rugby league was 'the most democratic game in the world', a belief that was reiterated on many occasions by its Antipodean followers. 'Rugby league, with justifiable pride, always emphasises the fact that it is the most democratic of sports,' proclaimed Sydney's *Rugby League News* in 1946.[20]

This close social affinity between sport in Australia and the north of England can be seen in the reactions to Australia of touring British rugby league teams.

The idea of Britain as 'home' was just as common in rugby league as it was in middle- and upper-class Australian culture. Eddie Waring was struck by the strength of the sentiment during the 1946 British tour of Australia and New Zealand: 'everyone calls England 'Home'. It is immaterial whether they have ever known anyone from the old country. It appears to be everyone's ambition to go 'home' and to hear youngsters with no English connections at all talking about 'home' - England - was truly remarkable.'[21]

But what is perhaps more noteworthy is the extent to which these feelings were reciprocated by British rugby league tourists to Australia. The manager of the 1932 British tour, Fred Hutchins, told a reception held in Sydney for the visitors that the tour 'is like coming home'. On tour four years earlier he had reported back to the British rugby league authorities that 'none of us are homesick'. Bob Anderton, Hutchins' joint manager on the 1932 tour, took this identification with Australia even further during an interview on Sydney's 2UE radio when he told listeners, 'I suppose you would all like to hear my impression of our bridge and our harbour,' referring to the Sydney Harbour Bridge that had been opened a few weeks before the tourists' arrival.[22]

Partly these sentiments were based on common feelings of British patriotism, as Harold Wagstaff, the captain of the 1920 British tourists, made clear when he called for Test matches to be played in 'the British spirit of sportsmanship, for we are Britishers of the old land and you are Britishers of the new land. We're all the same in blood and sport, and know how to lose and, I hope, how to win.'[23]

Similarly, at a dinner for the 1936 British tourists held in Brisbane, tour manager Bob Anderton recited an acrostic poem he had written, based on the name of the host city, which ended, 'A for the Anzacs who fought with such fame/N is our Nation of which we are proud/E for old England, let's cheer long and loud.' As he recorded in his letter home, both parties did indeed cheer long and loud.[24]

But there was another aspect of the British tourists' experience in Australia that caused them to feel so comfortable there: the apparent absence of the overt class discrimination that they faced in their own country. To some extent this was because rugby league was the dominant sport of NSW and Queensland and the tourists enjoyed a level of public interest that, outside of the game's heartlands in Cumberland, Lancashire and Yorkshire, was unattainable in England. But it was also due to what they perceived to be the egalitarianism of Australian society. Coming from the rigidly class-stratified society of Britain, the lack of social deference and hierarchy was highly noticeable. Even their experience of the sea voyage to Australia could be socially uncomfortable - the 1936 tourists changed from a two-class ship to a single-class ship for the journey back to Britain - but once ashore in Australia they found a society in which they felt themselves to be accepted as equals.

From the 1920s to the 1960s the tourists were regularly referred to as the 'chooms', a variation of the friendly Australian colloquialism 'chums' that denoted a recently-arrived immigrant, suitably adapted to reflect the broad northern English vowels of the visitors. Unlike in Britain, the reference to accent carried no social stigma. The fact that they were welcomed as national representatives also offered a degree of social esteem that was denied them at home - indeed, in 1924 *The Times* had even questioned the rugby league tourists' right to be called England, placing quotation marks around 'English' when describing the team.[25]

This change in their social status when in Australia was most noticeable when the tourists attended the many civic receptions and dinners that were held in their honour. The 1936 tour managers were not alone in being moved by the 'wonderful hospitality from the Government and Civic Authorities down to the humble citizen'.[26]

When the Australian Governor-General William McKell organised a reception for the 1950 tourists, the party was amazed to find that not only could he talk with great knowledge about rugby league but that he came from a similar social background, having been a boilermaker in Balmain. 'He sat and talked with us and in his presence we were quite at home and very much impressed', reported the tour manager George Oldroyd. This stood in marked contrast to their experiences at home, where the opportunities to talk to representatives of the monarchy or holders of high offices of state were effectively non-existent for the sport and its representatives - the highest ranking government official to meet with the British RFL up until the 1960s was actually an Australian, H.V. Evatt. As Oldroyd's comment implies, the rugby league tourists' sense of affinity with Australia was based as much on ideas of class equality as it was on notions of racial identity.[27]

This synthesis of working-class identity and imperial Britishness can also be see in the personal stories of those who ran the game.

In the late 1940s Harold 'Jersey' Flegg - president of the NSWRL from 1929 to his death in 1960 and arguably the most powerful administrator in the history of Australian league - was introduced by William McKell to Lord Macdonald, visiting from England. Mishearing the peer's name he greeted him: 'G'day Claude'. McKell corrected him: 'No Jerse, it's Lord, not Claude', to which Flegg responded, 'We don't go with that bullshit here. This is Australia'.

Yet, despite his refusal to doff his cap in deference to the British aristocracy, it was also Flegg who vehemently proclaimed his Britishness to the British tour managers in 1950 and who had refused to countenance a possible merger with Australian Rules in 1933 because of 'the British tone and atmosphere of rugby'.

The biographies of two of the early leaders of the sport also demonstrate how widespread was the holding of these two seemingly contradictory positions. Ted Larkin, a Catholic and an avowed socialist, enthusiastically enlisted in the army just two weeks following the outbreak of World War One. He met his death at Gallipoli. Even Jack Fihelly, possibly Brisbane's most noted anti-war campaigner in 1914-1918, was a model of decorum when, as acting Queensland premier, he welcomed the Prince of Wales to Queensland in 1920.[28]

From Chooms to Poms

As with so many aspects of the Anglo-Australian relationship, the ties that bound rugby league so closely together began to tear apart in the early 1960s.

The changing economic relationship between the two countries, the diplomatic consequences of decolonisation, the ending of free entry into Britain for all Commonwealth citizens, and the Macmillan government's application to join the European Common Market without consulting the Australian government led to growing Australian alienation from Britain. In rugby league, the traditional imperial relationship was transformed within a generation.

In 1946 and 1950 the British tourists had been treated as heroes. The NSWRL presented each member of the 1946 touring team with a food parcel worth one pound to take back home with them because, said the league's vice-president Frank Miller, 'we admire the way England took it, and is still taking it, and these men, and their families, know austerity as we never knew it'.

At a reception for the 1950 tourists at a Returned & Services League club in Brisbane they were welcomed with a speech in which, according to tour manager George Oldroyd, the chairman told them 'how they valued our contribution in the last war when we stood alone for one year and [how] Australia would have been in a poor plight but for our efforts'.[29]

But by the mid-sixties this attitude had almost completely disappeared. The tourists were no longer regarded as 'chooms' but as 'Poms', and even, on occasions, 'Pommie Bastards'.

The 1950s had seen a series of administrative disputes between the British and Australian leagues which reflected the changing economic strengths of the two bodies. The legalisation of poker machines in New South Wales in 1956 opened up extensive sources of revenue for rugby league clubs, which could now use gambling revenue from their associated leagues clubs to subsidise their on-field activities. Coupled with the abandonment of the residential qualification for players in 1959, which meant that players no longer had to live in the immediate catchment area of their club, and the development of a formal contract system, Sydney rugby league clubs were now able to compete financially with British clubs.

From the early 1960s British players began to take advantage of their football skills, and the assisted passage scheme, to emigrate and play in Sydney. Among the million or so British citizens who emigrated to Australia between 1947 and 1970 were a number of high profile rugby league players, bringing expertise to the Australian game and weakening the British. At the same time, the sharp decline of heavy industry in the North of England, traditionally the basis of rugby league support, led to a severe reduction in attendances that also undermined the strength of the sport.[30]

The changing balance of forces was highlighted in 1961 by an Australian threat to cancel the forthcoming 1962 tour by the British unless a more equitable division of the tour's revenue could be negotiated. To cancel a tour, hitherto seen as the cultural and economic lifeblood of the game, was an unprecedented threat. British attempts to play the imperial card were rebuffed.

Tom Mitchell, the manager of the 1958 British tour, unsuccessfully appealed to the Australian league authorities on the basis that 'agreement in sport should always be possible, *and between members of the Commonwealth family a certainty*' [emphasis in original]. Eventually a compromise was reached and the tour went ahead. Despite considerable

British success on the pitch, the tour was blighted by continuous off-field disputes, perhaps best encapsulated by an argument between the British tour manager Stuart Hadfield and an official of St. George leagues club which ended with Hadfield being told that 'you are a lot of English bastards'.[31]

In many ways this marked a watershed. Previous British tourists to Australia had been surprised, and perhaps shocked, at the common use of 'bastard' in everyday conversation but had always regarded it, in the words of Eddie Waring, as 'a means of affection' used between friends.[32] Certainly there are no reports of it being used in a hostile or aggressive manner during social or business events before the 1960s (although the same could not be said for players or spectators during matches). The fact that bastard was now invariably preceded by 'Pommie' (or conversely that 'Pom' invariably followed 'whinging') meant that terms hitherto generally seen as friendly were now viewed by Australians and British as being antagonistic and often confrontational. This rising sense of suspicion and hostility was highlighted most strongly in the Australian tabloid press, especially during the struggle between the *Sun* and the *Daily Mirror* in Sydney for afternoon supremacy in the 1960s.

By 1966 the use of 'Pommie' or 'Pommy' by the press to describe the British touring team of that year had become ubiquitous. Perhaps the most egregious example was in a series of interviews given to the Sydney *Daily Mirror* by the British tour manager Jack Errock, in which he allegedly stated that the actions of his Australian counterparts 'had made my Pommy blood boil' and that he would 'never tour Australia again'.

Over three days Errock complained about the rudeness of Australian officials, the bias of referees and the poor quality of the food he was served. The interviews created such a furore that the RFL held an inquiry into them when the touring party returned to Britain at which, as was to be expected, the blame was ascribed to the sensationalism of the Sydney press.[33]

Undoubtedly there was some truth in this allegation. But the articles were also a reflection of the changing attitudes of Australians towards the British, even towards those with whom they had traditionally shared some affinity. Errock had been portrayed by the press as a stereotypical 'whinging Pom' who disliked everything about Australia. What was more, he had appeared to embrace the characterisation by apparently describing himself as a 'Pommy', thus emphasising the antagonism between Britain and Australia. Every Englishman, it now seemed, was a potential Douglas Jardine.

This division had become a gulf by the 1970 British tour to Australia. Shortly after arriving the tourists were embroiled in controversy after a fight at a party in Brisbane involving Malcolm Reilly, who took exception to an Australian who had called him a 'Pommie bastard'. This rumbled on for weeks and culminated in Reilly's arrest in Sydney. Far from being seen as 'chooms', tour manager Jack Harding complained that the first Test match had been portrayed as a 'hate war' and that the players were being portrayed in the press as 'a beer swilling, pot-bellied lot'.[34]

In many ways, the working-class image of rugby league players also fitted with contemporary Australian tabloid stereotypes of immigrant British trade unionists who were held to be responsible for strikes and other industrial disputes. The idea of the whinging pom could apply equally to arrogant British managers or lazy unfit players.

These changes in attitude were also seen in the behaviour of Australian touring teams to Britain. For example, the 1967 tour was the last in which the Australians began each match with an aboriginal war cry. This was a custom which dated back to their first tour of Britain in 1908 when tour manager Jack Fihelly had taught the players a war cry, allegedly originating from Stradbroke Island, that had been performed by a troupe of Queensland aboriginal men before the NSWRL's first grand final.[35]

Although none of the tourists were of aboriginal descent, the practice had been continued both by rugby league and rugby union touring sides. In the broader context of colonial relations, the war cry symbolised the subservience of Australians to the Empire by emphasising their link with peoples viewed as 'primitive' and by seeking to highlight a sense of the exotic, but unquestionably inferior, otherness of the farthest reaches of the Empire. The ubiquity of aboriginal displays during royal visits to Australia highlighted this relationship between these non-threatening, tightly controlled displays and Imperial loyalty. In this it was very different from the embrace of aboriginal symbols by the 'new nationalism' that appeared in Australia from the late 1960s.

By the 1967 tour the war cry was viewed by the players as a joke and its performance as an occasion to make up their own words. It was not performed on the next tour of Britain in 1973.

The 1967 tour was also notable for highlighting the change in attitude of the players. No longer was the tour of Britain seen as a journey 'Home'. Off the field, it had become an occasion for ostentatious displays of larrikinism and drunkenness. Although there had been reports of players misbehaving on the 1959 tour of Britain, the 1967 tour is remembered in rugby league folklore less for its on-field action than for the 'man in the bowler hat' affair, in which an un-named player strolled through Ilkley wearing nothing but the aforementioned headgear. Hotels and pubs used by the team suffered extensive damage', resulting in two of the most senior players being fined A$250 and having so much of their tour bonus docked for breaches of discipline that they made no money at all from the trip.[36]

In the 1970s the relationship between rugby league in Australia and Britain changed fundamentally. As well as the end of deference towards Britain and the contrasting economic fortunes of the sport, the balance of power in the playing of game had tilted hugely in favour of the former junior partner.

The 1970 Test series was the last to be won by Britain. Between 1978 and 1988 the British did not win even a single Test match. This exacerbated the tendency that was exhibited in other sports, especially cricket, in which the focus of Australian sport shifted from the Anglo-Australian arena to a world stage. But the narrow international base of rugby league meant that in Australia the importance and intensity of Anglo-Australian Test matches was replaced by the annual NSW versus Queensland 'State of Origin' series, in which the same aggressive masculinity originally displayed against fellow British 'chooms' was now employed against fellow Australian 'mates'.

Conclusion

In many ways, rugby league could be described as the most 'Australian' of sports because it encapsulated the two seemingly contradictory attitudes of imperial loyalty and hostility to privilege.

Unlike the geographically-limited Australian Rules football and the unashamedly exclusive rugby union, Anglo-Australian rugby league Test matches provided an arena in which these attitudes could be displayed to the full.

Although they may seem to be mutually exclusive when viewed from a present day point of view, they were not.

Historically, just as the British Labour Party supported the monarchy and the Empire, the Australian Labour Party's White Australia policy was intertwined with racial pride in being British. Britishness did not necessarily have to be that of the southern English home counties or of conservative Australians. It could also be expressed in ways that were seemingly oppositional and egalitarian, at least for those with white skins.[37]

Indeed, when viewed through the perspective of working-class Britishness, one must also ask how distinctive was Australian sporting culture, and by extension popular culture itself?

Those sporting traits identified by historians in the 1960s and 1970s on closer inspection turn out to be little different from those displayed in the North of England. And, as the experience of rugby league tourists to Australia demonstrates, the similarities between society in the North and in Australia were such that the tourists possibly felt more at home in Sydney than they would have done in London. Again, this should come as no surprise. The millions of British immigrants to Australia came overwhelmingly from the working classes, and many of them explicitly sought a new life free of the ossified social restrictions of Britain while seeking to preserve those customs they valued at home.

The case of rugby league also highlights a problem that often arises when discussing concepts such as British identity. That is the assumption that Britishness is identical with the English upper- and middle-classes based in the south of England, embodied in sporting terms by the public school-educated, amateur captains of touring England cricket teams.

However, this dominant notion of Britishness was

sharply contested not only by the non-English nations of Britain but also within England itself. The idea of a democratic, meritocratic North of England free of privilege and patronage was a strong ideological factor not only in nineteenth century Liberal and twentieth century Labour politics but also especially within the popular culture of the North itself. Indeed, much of what has traditionally been seen as a distinctively Australian sporting character is not qualitatively different from the sporting culture of the industrial North of England.

No wonder that whether they were going from Britain to Australia or from Australia to Britain, rugby league tourists always felt that they were going home.[38]

Notes

[1] *Yorkshire Post*, 6 January 1930. *Sydney Sun*, 26 June 1932.

[2] The original version of this chapter was published as 'Australian nationalism and working-class Britishness in Australian rugby league football', *History Compass*, 3 (April 2005) AU 142. I am grateful to the Council of Australian State Libraries for awarding me a fellowship in 2004 that allowed me to conduct much of the research for this article at the Mitchell Library in Sydney.

[3] W.F. Mandle, 'Cricket and Australian Nationalism in the Nineteenth Century' *Journal of the Royal Australian Historical Society*, vol. 59, no. 4, 1973.

[4] Sean Fagan, *The Rugby Rebellion*, Sydney, 2006.

[5] For more on the links between rugby league and the Australian labour movement see Andrew Moore, 'Opera of the Proletariat: Rugby League, the Labour Movement and Working-Class Culture in New South Wales and Queensland', *Labour History*, No. 79 (November 2000), pp. 57-70.

[6] Edmund Scott, *Rugby League in Brisbane: from the Genesis to the Formation of the Brisbane Rugby League*, unpublished Masters thesis, Human Movement, University of Queensland, 1990.

[7] *Referee*, 23 June 1910. Quoted in Robert Gate, *The Struggle for the Ashes*, Ripponden, 1986, p. 20. New South Wales Rugby League minutes, 12 July 1954.

[8] Undated interview with Alf Ellaby, cassette tape, (Rugby Football League Archives, Leeds). Corbett, *Sydney Sun*, 26 June 1932. Fallowfield quoted in Churchill, *Little Master*, p. 145. Ray Stehr, *Sydney Sun*, 7 May 1958.

[9] Gavin Souter, *Lion and Kangaroo: The Initiation of Australia*, Sydney, revised edition 2000, p. 357.

[10] *Rugby League News* (Sydney), 12 June 1926. *Sydney Morning Herald*, 27 May 1910, Sunderland quoted in the diary of Harold Bowman in M. Ullyatt and D. Bowman (eds), *Harold Bowman on Tour Down Under*, Beverley, 1992, p. 13. Letter from City Tattersall's Club to E. Osborne, 25 July 1928 (RFL Archives). RFL Council minutes, 10 October 1945.

[11] Australian Rugby League Board of Control minutes, 21 July 1950. RFL Council minutes, 18 November 1954. Ron Lock and Peter Quantrill, *Zulu Victory*, London, 2003. *Truth* quoted in Bennet Manson, *Another Battle for Britain*, Altrincham, 1958, p. 58.

[12] Mandle, 'Cricket and Australian Nationalism', p. 241, and also his *Going It Alone. Australia's National Identity in the Twentieth Century*, Melbourne, 1978, p. 31.

[13] See Dave Russell, 'Sport and identity: the case of Yorkshire County Cricket Club, 1890-1939', *Twentieth Century British History* (1996) 7, 2.

[14] *Yorkshireman*, 1 October 1890.

[15] See, for example, Richard Cashman, '*Ave a go, yer mug!': Australian cricket crowds from larrikin to ocker*, Sydney, 1984.

[16] McKivat quoted in Ian Heads, *The Kangaroos - The saga of rugby league's great tours*, Sydney, 1990, p. 41. Clive Churchill, *They called me the Little Master*, Sydney, 1962, p. 67.

[17] *Athletic News*, 28 February 1910.

[18] Graham McInnes, *The Road to Gundagai*, London (Second Edition), 1985, p. 72.

[19] *Rugby League News* (Sydney), 7 June 1941.

[20] Undated press clipping (c. July 1914) in JC Davis collection, box 51, item 4, Mitchell Library, Sydney. For Australian usage of 'the people's game' see, for example, *Rugby League News* (Sydney), 29 May 1926. Eddie Waring, *England to Australia and New Zealand*, Leeds, 1947, p. 5. *Rugby League News* (Sydney), 4 May 1946.

[21] J.F. O'Loghlen (ed.) *Rugby League Annual and Souvenir*, Sydney, 1928, p. 108. Waring, *England to Australia and New Zealand*, p. 85.

[22] *Rugby League News* (Sydney) 28 May, 1932. G.F. Hutchins letter to John Wilson 13 July 1928 (RFL Archives). *Rugby League News* (Sydney) 4 June 1932.

[23] Harold Wagstaff speech at Sydney Town Hall, *Referee*, 2 June 1920.

[24] Letter from R.F. Anderton to John Wilson, 6 July 1936 (RFL Archives).

[25] Waring, *England to Australia and New Zealand*, p. 33. *The Times*, 30 September 1924.

[26] *1936 Tour to Australia and New Zealand Report* (undated). See also the letter from G.F. Hutchins to John Wilson, 18 June 1928 (RFL Archives).

[27] *1936 Tour to Australia and New Zealand Report*. George Oldroyd, *1950 Tour Business Manager's Report* (undated). (RFL Archives). While an apprentice boilermaker in 1901, McKell had helped train the future Australian rugby league captain and coach Rick Johnston as a riveter in a shipyard. *Rugby League News* (Sydney), 17 June 1946.

[28] Quoted in Moore, 'Opera of the proletariat', *Labour History*, p. 64. *Referee*, 3 August 1933.

[29] *Rugby League News* (Sydney) 18 May 1946. George Oldroyd, *1950 Tour Business Manager's Report*.

[30] Andrew Moore, *The Mighty Bears, A social history of North Sydney rugby league*, Sydney, 1996, pp. 290-8. British considerations in 1957 can be seen in the minutes of the RFL Council, 10 October 1957.

[31] Tom Mitchell, *Memorandum on 1962 Tour*, 15 November 1961, (RFL Archives). Stuart Hadfield to RFL Council, 9 July 1962.

[32] Eddie Waring, *England to Australia and New Zealand*, Leeds, 1947, p. 23.

[33] The articles are reprinted in the minutes of the RFL Council meeting, 21 December 1966.

[34] J.B. Harding, *Australian Tour 1970 - First Report*, (undated), p. 7, *Australian Tour 1970 - Fourth Report*, 24 June 1970, p. 2 (RFL Archives).

[35] The background is detailed in the *Sydney Morning Herald*, 29 August 1908.

[36] RFL Council minutes, 3 January and 22 February 1968. Heads, *The Kangaroos*, pp. 177-9 and pp. 215-8.

[37] Jonathan Hyslop, 'The Imperial Working Class Makes Itself "White": White Labourism in Britain, Australia and South Africa before the First World War', *Journal of Historical Sociology*, 12 (1999), pp. 398-421.

[38] For a comprehensive and outstanding discussion of northern English identity, see Dave Russell, *Looking North: Northern England and the national imagination*, Manchester, 2004. For links between the North of England and Australia see Andrew Moore, 'Yorkshireness and Australia: some preliminary observations', *Journal of Regional and Local Studies*, vol. 21, no. 2, (Summer/Winter 2001) pp.49-5.

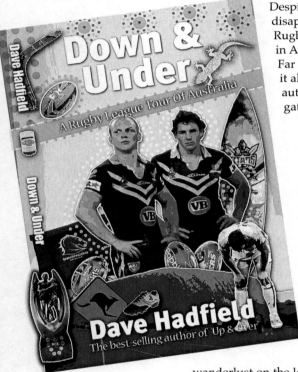

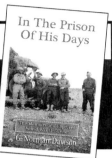

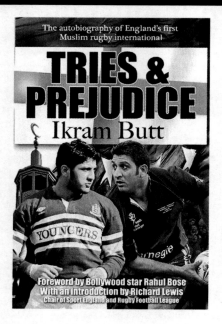

The autobiography of England's first Muslim rugby international

TRIES & PREJUDICE
Ikram Butt

YOUNGERS

rnegie

Foreword by Bollywood star Rahul Bose
With an introduction by Richard Lewis
Chair of Sport England and Rugby Football League

In February 1995, Ikram Butt became England's first Muslim rugby international in either code - blazing a trail for British Asians.

Since then, the former Leeds, Featherstone, London, Huddersfield and Hunslet rugby league star has continued to campaign for wider Asian involvement in sport and in 2004 was a prime mover in the formation of BARA - the British Asian Rugby Association. From the start, BARA had a vital social as well as sporting function. How could it not, in the wake of such 'War on Terror'-related atrocities as 9/11, 7/7 and the reported alienation of Britain's disaffected Asian youth?

Now, for the first time, Ikram Butt has his say, telling of his upbringing in Headingley; his own experiences on the wrong end of the law; the potential conflict between personal ambition and religion; racism in sport; run-ins with coaches and short-sighted officials; and, most recently, his regular visits to the House of Commons and pioneering development work in the UK, India and Pakistan.

Tries & Prejudice is by turns amusing, controversial, humane and eye-opening. It provides long overdue food for thought for politicians, the public and sports governing bodies alike.   ISBN 978-0956007537

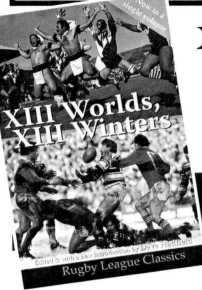

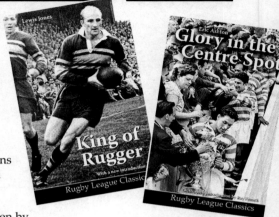